With Justice for All

The Investigation of a 54-Sense Organic Technology of Behavior

The astonishing transcript of a grand jury inquest into how a key federal agency's omission of Nature's ways, in and around us, violates our human and constitutional rights. The testimony of its witnesses spotlights the politically suppressed art and science of Albert Einstein's unifying field, a holistic, 54-sense, conflict resolution process whose honesty strengthens personal, social and environmental well-being.

E PLURIBUS UNUM

Project NatureConnect

Michael J. Cohen, Ed.D., Ph.D.
Director

CreateSpace.com **for Project NatureConnect**.net
Warrantied GreenWave-54 whole life science and relationships.
P. O. Box 1605 Friday Harbor WA 98250   (360) 378-6313
www.ecopsych.com nature@interisland.net

Updated from *Educational Transformation: The university as catalyst for human advancement* published by Akamai University, 2016. Chapter 3, *With Justice For All,* Michael J. Cohen.
© 2016 Michael J. Cohen

Note: this book with its links active is available online free at www.ecopsych.com/grandjury.html

BOOK TOPIC

It is well established that our disturbing psycho-emotional experiences underlie our greatest personal and social problems. This book represents a transcript of the U.S. Department of Justice Grand Jury convened to make available Albert Einstein's unifying GreenWave, 54 sense, art and science of Education, Counseling and Healing with Nature (GreenWave-54). This whole-life tool is a suppressed organic antidote for most problems and it is illegally being withheld from the public in violation of human rights including those in the First and Fourteenth Amendments of the U.S. Constitution. This misconduct is significant because to reasonably heal our injured 54 natural senses and the life of Planet Earth, GreenWave-54 therapeutically reconnects these senses to their self-correcting origins in the natural world, backyard or backcountry. This corrects the illusions that disrupt our balance and produce our disorders. In the inquest the Grand Jury learns about the error of using nature-substitute remedies for our runaway problems instead of invoking the GreenWave-54 process. This is like taking a broken computer to a blacksmith for repairs while in denial that a blacksmith's expertise is inappropriate for computer maintenance, in fact his repair job months earlier injured it and that's why it doesn't work now.

AUTHOR

Applied Ecopsychologist Michael J. Cohen

While developing the GreenWave-54 process since 1953 Mike has achieved several Master's and Doctoral degrees, written 11 books, directed sensory organic university environmental education and outdoor education courses and degree programs for over 50 years as well as, for decades, developed and lived outdoors on year-long, "utopian community," environmental education expeditions. He is recognized as a Maverick Genius and has received the Distinguished World Citizen award for his contributions. He conceived the 1985 symposium 'Is the Earth a Living Organism' and has experientially solved Albert Einstein's Unified Field Equation. Mike founded and directs Project NatureConnect. He warranties its accuracy as well as guarantees its quality because it consists of sweeping, self-evident facts of life that include our 54 natural senses. Although scrutinized since 1982, these 54 facts have yet to be denied.

Table of Contents

Preface

Scientific research is based on the idea that everything that takes place is determined by laws of nature, and therefore this holds for the action of people.

Our task must be to free ourselves from our prison by widening our circles of compassion to embrace all living creatures and the whole of nature in its beauty.

- Albert Einstein

Responses to "Why is Albert Einstein's GreenWave Unified Field Equation significant?"

"It helps 'I want to make a difference' become 'I have a tool that enables me to make a difference"

It lets us express love through acts that make our words trustable and our disorders subside.

"This social technology powerfully helps people reduce their conflicts and realize inner peace."

It's a free, doable way to tap into Nature's fountainhead of authority in producing its wisdom.

"Substantiates natural systems theory with repeatable, first hand, experiences and observations."

To establish a peaceful and sane world, we must, require every leader and parent to master this equation. It could correctly be called 'Earth's OK, I'm OK' or 'Romancing Our Planet.'

"It sounds like it describes the workings of another universe until our experiences show us it is part of the life of Earth and ourselves that we seldom get to see."

Scientifically engages us in a holistic 54 sense process where attractions in nature unify our conflicted natural senses and stories. It's the missing glue that we need for unification.

"Its discovery is more useful than e=mc² because it frees the values of wilderness within us. This helps our 54 sense inner nature recover its integrity while it helps the life of Earth do the same."

Makes accessible presently missing information and energies in natural areas that we need to create personally and globally sound relationships.

"Gives rise to the internet becoming a courier for embracing Earth's self-correcting energies."

This invaluable educational tool enables me to transform irresponsible social and environmental elements of society into constructive planetary citizenship relationships.

"Presents the means for us to recover our soul by restoring Nature's ways in our consciousness."

Gives me an ally in nature that helps me help students improve their learning abilities.

"By heightening all my 54 natural senses it saved me ten trips to the psychiatrist.

Introduction

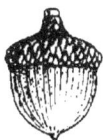 **A Technology of Behavior,** 1971
Edited and extended from *Beyond Freedom and Dignity* by B.F. Skinner (Skinner, 1971)

"In trying to solve the terrifying problems that faced us in 1971, we naturally turned to the things we did best. We played and still play from strength, and our strength is science and technology.

- To contain a population explosion, we look for better methods of birth control.
- To decrease mental illness, we seek more powerful drugs and therapies. that provide stronger and more lasting satisfactions.
- Threatened by a nuclear holocaust, we build bigger deterrent forces, internet espionage and anti-ballistic missile systems.
- We try to stave off world famine with new foods and better ways of growing them.
- Improved sanitation and medicine will, we hope, control disease, better housing and transportation will solve the problems of the ghettos,
- New ways of reducing or disposing of waste will stop the pollution of the environment.
- Alternative energy sources will replace fossil fuels and reduce climate change.

We can point to remarkable achievements in all these fields since 1971, and it is not surprising that we should try to extend them. But as the catastrophic excessiveness of Earth Overshoot Day in 2016 A.D. demonstrates, things have grown steadily worse and it is disheartening to find that our emotionally dependent attachment to objective science and technology is increasingly at fault.

- Sanitation and medicine have made the problems of population more acute,
- War has acquired more horror with the invention of new nuclear weapons,
- The affluent pursuit of happiness is largely responsible for pollution.
- The excessive use of drugs has addicted us to them as well as produced increasing immunity to their benefits.
- The high tech, non-organic satisfactions of our wants produces emotional instability and environmental deterioration.
- Inexpensive alternative energy increases consumerism and economic

Growth and development accompanied by greater Earth misery.
- We continue to excessively sense, feel and act as if contemporary society is not part of, embedded in and affected by the health of our planet's life.

The application of physical, biological and social sciences alone will not solve our problems because the solutions lie in another field. What we need is an *organic technology of behavior* presently missing in our activities and disciplines. We will solve our problems when we can use sensory organics to adjust the growth of the world's population and its destructive ways as precisely as we adjust the course of a spaceship.

Earth Overshoot Day, August 27, 2011, 41 years after the publication of Skinner's *Beyond Freedom*, this date is when Planet Earth ran out of resources for the rest of the year 2011 to support humanity. During these years our scientists and leaders have not made a technology or tool available to deal  with our excessiveness and the miseries it creates. Our destructive resource use, disorders and discontents of 1971 have risen 45 percent, on average, with no end to this trend in sight. Half the species present in 1971 are extinct now while mental illness has doubled and most discontents increased. We need another Planet Earth half the size of Earth to connect with and return to balanced wellness. Nobody knows the point source of this dilemma, where this extra planet can be found or how to connect it with Earth.

Earth Overshoot Day, August 22, 2012. With the discovery of the Higgs Boson natural attraction field announced in July, the source of our life support catastrophe and the remedy for it was affirmed by Project NatureConnect. The source is that contemporary society is in denial. We deny that we addictively educate ourselves to limited and misleading science and technology stories that motivate us to fight an undeclared war against the life of Nature and Earth. We lose this fight as we win it since these stories support our conquest of Nature moment-by-moment and with the exception of our nature-disconnected stories we are part of Nature. We deny that the remedy for this tragedy is a 54 sense, advanced behavioral technology, the *Albert Einstein Unified Field Equation whole life art and science of GreenWave educating, counseling and healing with Nature* (**GreenWave-54**).

Earth Overshoot Day, August 8, 2016: A investigative Federal Grand Jury is planned because we need laws to protect our legal rights to use the GreenWave-54 process that connects our body mind and spirit to the self-correcting ways of the natural world in and around us. Without it, our human and civil rights are being violated. Since 1983, GreenWave-54 Organic Psychology has been available yet negligently withheld by the US Department of Education. *With Justice for All* contains the Grand Jury transcript and how to implement the facts presented to the Jurors.

With Justice for All

In order to change an existing paradigm, you do not struggle to try and change the problematic model. You create a new model and make the old one obsolete.

- **Robert Buckminister Fuller**

Synopsis

This 2016 transcript is the projected text of a United States Department of Justice Grand Jury that will convene to investigate the U.S. Department of Education and Higher Education Accrediting Associations. It provides indisputable evidence that for decades they have violated constitutional human rights by withholding the conflict resolution, fact finding process of Albert Einstein's 54 Sense GreenWave Unified Field Equation (GreenWave-54) that produces well-being through education, counseling, and healing with Nature. GreenWave-54 consists of self-evidence, of undeniable, sensory experiences in natural areas that remedy the source of most problems and are more true and practical than knowing that the sun will rise tomorrow. GreenWave-54 helps us stop the dangerous natural resource deficiency that contemporary society continues to produce, one whose miseries increasingly deteriorate the life of Planet Earth and our body, mind, and spirit. (Project Nature Connect, PNC, 2012a). *(Our 54 senses are identified in this book's Appendix, page 82. Ed.)*

This investigation equally applies to the U.S Department of Health and Human Services for its similar violations of human rights and environmental justice. It is critically important because at every level the absence of GreenWave-54 reduces organically sound personal, social and environmental well-being while increasing our vulnerability to individual and global corruption and the whole-life disorders that their trespasses create.

A Transcript of the GreenWave-54 Grand Jury Testimony

The opening statement of Robert Goldwater starts this document. He is the Prosecutor from the U.S. Department of Justice for a Grand Jury to investigate a class action complaint (Plaintiffs) against both the U.S. Department of Education and Higher Education Accrediting Associations (Defendants). Federal, state and local governments depend upon the Defendants to fulfill their responsibilities to all parties concerned.

Prosecutor Robert Goldwater's Opening Statement

Good Morning, Jury members. Thank you for fulfilling your duties as American citizens to help justice for all prevail through trial by judge and jury. The Plaintiffs have filed with the U.S. Department of Justice, a class action complaint against the Defendants, individually and in collusion, for breaching a wide range of the human and civil rights of the Plaintiffs.

The core of this complaint is that as one of nine planets that orbit the sun, the life of Planet Earth has its own profound life-giving qualities and integrity, an essence that is shared and depended upon by all members of Earth's web-of-life including humanity. When human offenders negligently deteriorate the life of Earth, they violate the guaranteed legal and inalienable rights of each of us to our survival, health, property and the quality of our life. This is unjust and wrong. The offenders are liable for this alleged offense as well as responsible for correcting it.

This complaint results from the Defendants' denial and carelessness in meeting their responsibility to incorporate and implement the legitimate facts and unifying methods and materials that enable education in the United States to meet minimum standards that insure the life and health guaranteed to all citizens by the Constitution. This defies the rules of our First, Fifth and Fourteenth Amendments that guarantee free speech, life, liberty and property protection. To this end, and in good faith as a Prosecutor for the Department of Justice, I have investigated and selected critical topics that sworn-in, expert witnesses will present for you to weigh as evidence.

I have, along with some Plaintiffs and experts, questioned the witnesses so that here this morning they may each make a short statement that presents an overview of their observations and findings. This will allow Jurors to better understand the further testimony of the witnesses this afternoon as well as question them with regard to the

Plaintiffs' allegations. I will advise you on the relevance of the evidence and on the law as will Judge Marilyn Wilson when necessary.

I have drafted the charges fairly and they will show that you must indict the Defendants so a judge and jury may properly settle this injustice later by rule of law where the Defendants may be heard. Please note that an additional Plaintiff here, one that all the class action Plaintiffs hold in common, will not be present now and in the possible forthcoming trial. This is because that Plaintiff has no rights or legal standing in the eyes of the law. *(I have included here that plaintiff, the life of Nature, by including its pictures on these pages, Ed.)*

I have asked the Witnesses to express their knowledge and views using information that can also be found on the Internet so that the Jurors can see that it is common knowledge, not private or restricted, and that the Defendants had full access to it as well as the responsibility and authority to require its use and distribute it. This information is available as well for any Juror. You can locate it in a search engine through its topics.

For greater completeness I have asked each Witness to cite individuals not present whose statements support their testimony. For example, if the real, alive Albert Einstein was on the witness stand rather than just someone who could convey some of his knowledge, the impact and outcome of the testimony would produce greater impact from the same information. Sources for their quotes are available via Internet search engines. I have also asked each witness to summarize what their testimony contributes and that it be included in the transcript of these proceedings.

You 23 Jurors along with additional online Jurors must decide whether the evidence presented by the witnesses shows due cause for this case to proceed to court so appropriate liabilities, fines, punishments, and a Judge may take necessary steps in this regard. To this end, and with respect to its responsibility to the American people, the Justice Department last month convened a committee of recognized experts in appropriate fields. They vetted all the witnesses listed by the Plaintiffs and myself and with due diligence they selected to present facts to this Grand Jury only from (a) witnesses with the strongest qualifications in their area of expertise who (b) had the greatest preponderance of evidence beyond reasonable doubt for their testimony along with (c) the most unblemished records for abiding by the law and (d) swearing or guaranteeing to tell the truth, the whole truth, and nothing but the truth. The witnesses have been kept separated and are unaware of each other's testimony.

The 23 of you have been selected as a fair cross section of society because with respect to the claims of the Plaintiffs, your charge is for you to be reasonable, to evaluate, and to blend from the wide range of your own personal education and life experiences, the fairness, appropriateness, well-being, and truth that you find in the testimony of each witness. This will challenge you since you have been educated, indoctrinated and put in denial by the Defendants and this influences how you see and relate to any situation. *In this way, you are also their victims.* This morning you are to pay attention to what scientifically has proven itself correct and makes the most sense to you in this complaint. This hearing will then examine further details this afternoon and tomorrow when we will bring the Witnesses back for full information and questioning

Jurors must know that they are considering for the Justice Department at this time, only a limited number of rights that have allegedly been violated. If you decide to send this case to trial, the Department will hold additional inquests into other rights that have also alleged to be violated. In these future hearings the prosecution will subpoena the most influential members of society to appear. This will assure that their power is brought to protect the people through these witnesses' areas of influence as well as through the Justice system.

The central issue of this hearing is that the civil and human rights of the Plaintiffs have been breached through undue prejudice and negligence. This is because the Defendants have had the opportunity to provide, but irresponsibly neglected to provide, federal government and private non-profit research, information, and educational services that the defendants are contracted to make available for the public good. Because we undeniably live in the time and space of the life of our planet, Earth and its integrity, when negligence by some parts of our society damages its health and property, they damage the health and property of others who depend upon Earth's health and resilience, including us. The offenders can be held legally responsible for their acts by those whose rights have been violated. Already in 2016 A.D., several suits have been filed against irresponsible corporations for damages and illness that has incurred from unabated climate change. These suits are presently in the process of trial by jury (Haulthaus, 2016, Block 2016).

The Defendants here are alleged to have fraudulently reduced public health and welfare through their omission of the scientifically valid Albert Einstein Unified Field 54-Sense Equation (GreenWave-54 or Einstein-54), and the process of Educating, Counseling, and Healing With Nature (ECHN). These social technologies include the Natural Attraction Ecology Model (PNC, 2007B) also known in some circles as Organic Psychology and the Natural Systems Thinking Process ("Natural Attraction Ecology," 2003). Hereinafter they all will collectively be referred to as GreenWave-54 or ECHN.

GreenWave-54 does the seemingly impossible. It validates that we have 54 natural sense attractions and each is conscious of what it is attracted to. They are part of Albert Einstein's Unified Field of the Big Bang Universe, that we call Nature, so our senses register it as themselves and they are guided by it in natural areas (Cohen, 2013). This strengthens by 85 percent peoples' organic ability to come out of denial and unify their personal lives with others, society, and the environment. It helps folks apply the high tech ways of objective science to 54 often conquered or blocked, subjective sensory facts (Cohen, 2014). These truths ordinarily produce the value and beauty of whole life relationships in balance, locally and globally (Albert Einstein, 2014). By using 54 rather than just 8 natural senses GreenWave-54 increases personal, social and environmental well-being by 85 percent at every level of endeavor. This decreases the costs of coping with the disorders caused by the deterioration of personal and global wellness due to our excessive disconnection from Nature (Cohen, 2015).

While this inquest is convened, during breaks Jurors are welcome to examine any detail of GreenWave-54 at its website **www.mjcnow.info**. I will officially introduce you to it later, but will demonstrate it process as part of this morning's session

The Defendants were paid and trusted to make the special contribution of GreenWave-54 to society. Because they failed to do this, the Plaintiffs demand reparations for health, life, and livelihood losses they have suffered, penalties for corrupt and unreasonable practices by the Defendants, and the enactment of new acts and laws that reverse as well as restore the damages that have been and are still being inflicted daily on them. These include the Defendant's effects on the U.S Department of Health and Human Services that make it liable for its violation of human rights and environmental justice.

The Witnesses will explain to you the Plaintiffs' case mostly using self-evidence or empirical evidence from GreenWave-54. This inquest will benefit from unified scientific facts, reasonable thinking and rational passion. These are not being enacted or are being disregarded by the Defendants in their contracted duties to promote excellence in education. Witnesses are aware they are liable for perjury and will be prosecuted, fined or up to 5-years imprisoned for presenting false testimony. As U. S. Attorney General Jeff Sessions has said, "People will surprise you how sometimes they'll just spill the beans when they're under oath."

Opening Statements of Witnesses

The Measurement of Earth's Carrying Capacity

WITNESS 1 Harold Dorn
GreenWave-54 Testimony

What is commonly called Earth Overshoot Day or Earth Misery Day has increased each year since 1975. This day marks the annual date when humanity exhausts Nature's resources on planet Earth. It signifies that all year long, since 1975, we, personally and planet-wise, have produced, registered and sensed an increasing natural resource deficiency, an emptiness, an unexplainable, discomforting void that eviscerates the whole life integrity of body, mind, spirit and environmental quality (The State of Planet Earth and Us, 2001). Its destructive source along with its remedy, although known for decades, has yet to be offered and integrated by educators because they are not required to acknowledge or include GreenWave-54 in their curriculums. Meanwhile, in 2015 we are operating at 145% greater resource use than our planet can provide yearly and this along with the misery factors it produces increases every year. Now, to come into balance with Earth we need an additional planet half the size of Earth to connect with and restore the capacity of Earth's integrity to stop, rather than continue to diminish, the quality of life and health of its biosphere and populations. Based on the environmental impact of the United States, we would need four additional planets to make up this alarming deficit. As Henry David Thoreau noted, *The price of anything is the amount of life you exchange for it,* (Searls, 2009).

We are each part of and suffer from our global deficit problem as well as benefit from its solution for we are part of Nature.

WITNESS 1 SUMMARY: by 85% GW-54 improves the quality, rights and well-being of life.

The least movement is of importance to all nature. The entire ocean is affected by a pebble.

- Blaise Pascal

The Integrity and Connectedness of the Global Life Community

WITNESS 2 Jennifer Long
GreenWave-54 Testimony

As an edited letter by Chief Seattle states, "All things are connected like the blood that unites us all. Man did not weave the web of life he is merely a strand in it. Whatever he does to the web, he does to himself" (Fishman, 1854).

The form and process of any single individual or environmental system is connected to everything else on Earth. As demonstrated by the complete recycling every few years of all the atoms in the human body, all life is connected to being a contributing and cooperating part to how the whole life of Earth works and vice versa. Every living thing survives by relationships with every other living thing and their environmental intimacy. All things are intertwined in a complex web of hidden and subtle relationships. Any one form of life depends on the rest of a life community to provide the conditions needed for its existence. For example, similar to our fingers being connected to our heart and toes, insecticides applied on Canadian crops end up in Antarctic penguins.

Like an approaching meteor that can be stopped by GreenWave-54, the sixth great mass extinction happening now is being caused by humanity not using GreenWave-54. Over 50% of species have disappeared because local and global extinction is now up to 1000 times the natural background rate (Kluger, 2014). As present symptoms show, this loss threatens ecosystem services of food and water, flood and disease control and our spiritual, aesthetic, recreational, and emotional demands along with nutrient recycling and carbon storage. These are all part of life. Our morals, ethics, and values must direct us to care about the fact that, on average, we spend over 95% of our time indoors and 99% of our felt-sense thinking and relationships out of tune with the natural world and its self-balancing ways around and within us. The loss and wanting, conscious or subconscious, of this separation from Nature's love deteriorates our normal ability to give and receive love. It feels too risky. This loss makes us demand excessive substitute fulfillments from Earth's resources. We are brainwashed to uncomfortably sense that we need more of everything. For example, no matter how rich or poor we are, we believe we need 15% more money. As if we are insane, we are bankrupting our natural economy and resources along with our body, mind, and spirit. We must use existing rescue packages that work before it is too late.

The methods and materials of GreenWave-54 help us remedy our increasing resource and love deficit. They empower us to genuinely connect our undisputed 54 natural attraction senses with the life of nature's unified field in and around us to recycle our injured and depleted senses and sensibilities. This enables our senses to become conscious of nature's callings. Like a "wisdom glue" it lets our consciousness of the Unified Field compost the pollution of our psyche so the unifying ways of the natural world can transform our education to promote rather than withhold GreenWave-54.

Consider this example: The sense and sensation of Thirst is as real and true a fact of life as is water itself. Thirst is a natural intelligence, a love that is conscious of its attraction to signal us when we need to connect with the global water cycle and bring water into us for our survival and to cleanse us. When we have enough water, Thirst is conscious of its attraction to turn itself off and it does. Later, the sense and sensation of Excretion is conscious of its attraction to tell us to release the water and our poisonous waste products from our body and, as if miraculously, they are exactly the correct food to feed the Web-of-Life as it purifies our excreted water.

What is true for our sense of thirst is equally true for our additional 53 sense groups (see Appendix) including the senses of Consciousness, Reason and Literacy (Cohen, 2014).

I go to nature to be soothed and healed, and to have my senses put in order.
- John Burroughs

 Today, the Educating, Counseling and Healing With Nature process (ECHN) based on Albert Einstein's Unified Field Equation (Cohen, 2013) may be the only scientific program available that works to make the unchangeable change. It successfully addresses our extreme 54 natural sense estrangement from our Planet as being a habit or psychological/psychiatric denial or an addiction problem or an emotional attachment disease that we can remedy (Cohen, 2009a).

Our 54 senses are the tools we use to register, love, believe and relate to the world. When they are lost or distorted nothing can be trusted.

The process of GreenWave-54 works simply because our excessive disconnections from Einstein's Unified Field makes us eviscerate the integrity of our planet and selves and produce our disorders. This is why our genuine reconnections with the Unified Field remedy them. In this sense GreenWave-54 is hope in action.

WITNESS 2 SUMMARY: by 85% GW-54 strengthens our ability to make beneficial changes.

We are like islands in the sea, separate on the surface but connected in the deep.
- William James

Personal Field Journal Report: **Equality and Love**

WITNESS 3 Stanley Farrel
GreenWave-54 Testimony:

I was thinking about my right to equality and my love of it as many of my colleagues returned from their walk on campus discontent at the school's lack of nature and the limitation of space to walk around as others have elsewhere. My reasoning mind could have agreed with them but my new, whole-life, sensory way of knowing could not. I experienced unified GreenWave-54 non-verbal awareness and nature's intelligence found me. I felt more at peace, connected, and open. Without addressing the questions for this GreenWave-54 assignment I would not have understood the entire connection as deeply as I do now. I have repeated it many times and it opens and softens me further when I do. I look forward to retrieving more of these experiences from where I have learned to store them, my mind, where they will remain intact and strong for my use at will. This makes me feel very connected, happy, and real. Our lives can't afford to be missing it.

WITNESS 3 SUMMARY: by 85% GW-54 enhances equality through wholeness.

> *Equality is the soul of liberty; there is, in fact, no liberty without it.*
> - **Frances Wright**

Education and Citizenship

WITNESS 4 Arnold Raquette
GreenWave-54 Testimony

The Defendants have harmfully omitted that, as John Dewey said, "The purpose of education has always been to everyone, in essence, the same—to give the young the things they need in order to develop in an orderly, sequential way to become contributing and wholesome members of society. To develop into a member of society what was needed in ancient times has almost nothing in common with developing into a member of society with what is needed in the advanced science and technology of today and its effects. To maintain and support well-being any education and its methods and materials, is an outgrowth of the needs of the society and the environment in which it exists" (Dewey, 1934). GreenWave-54 is an important contribution in this regard and the Defendants are negligent in their legal duties to make it available in all areas by including it as a required part of higher education.

WITNESS 4 SUMMARY: by 85% GW-54 mandates the appropriateness of education.

Democracy cannot succeed unless those who express their choice are prepared to choose wisely. The real safeguard of democracy, therefore, is education.

- Franklin D. Roosevelt

The U.S. Department of Education

WITNESS 5 James Darnell

GreenWave-54 Testimony:

Amongst many things the purpose of the United States Department of Education includes getting information on what works in education to teachers and education policymakers for the improvement of science, mathematics, and environmental instruction in elementary and secondary schools, graduate fellowships, and vocational-technical training. The department is required to raise national and community awareness of the education challenges confronting the Nation, to disseminate the latest discoveries on what works in teaching and learning, and to help communities work out solutions to difficult educational issues by increasing student achievement and preparation for global cooperation and competitiveness, fostering educational excellence and ensuring equal access. GreenWave-54 makes an important contribution in this regard because it enables education to include scientific truths concerning relating through natural attraction/love and its benefits. The Department of Education is irresponsible in not insisting that universities that receive federal dollars and offer federal financial assistance to students be required to teach it.

WITNESS 5 SUMMARY: by 85% GW-54 reinforces the scientific truth of natural love.

> *We have repressed far more than our sexuality: our very organic nature is now unconscious to most of us, most of the time, and we have become shrunken into two dimensional social or cultural beings, aware of only five of the hundreds of senses that link us to the rich biological nature that underlies and nourishes these more symbolic and recent aspects of ourselves.*
>
> — **Norman Brown**

The Legality of Regional Accrediting Associations

WITNESS 6 Samantha Roswell
GreenWave-54 Testimony:

Regional accrediting helps evaluate and ensure higher education's contribution to the common good and address the needs of society and students because it is a fundamental human right to which freedom of inquiry and expression are integral. Accreditation serves as the common unifying denominator of shared values and practices among diverse institutions. At its core are such questions as: What are students learning? Is it the right kind of learning? What difference is the institution making in their lives? What evidence does an institution have that ensures it is worth the student's investment?

Considering the already experienced effects of our increasing overuse of Earth's resources, it is hypocritical for accrediting associations to decide such questions and set the standards for federal financial assistance for students while omitting the unifying value of GreenWave-54 from their decisions as well as for to the common good. Before the U.S. Department of Education was set up, degrees were accepted for federal assistance if four other accredited schools recognized them. Today that option is gone and in addition U.S. financial aid to students is paying their tuitions to Wall Street sponsored Universities. The latter are making profits from payments by taxpayer-backed student loans. This is just another form of the underlying corrupt relationships that separate us from nature, in and around us. They result from the missing love and support from Nature that we suffer and that GreenWave-54 helps us recover. An analysis of current accreditation would conclude that institutional purposes, rather than public purposes, predominate.

WITNESS 6 SUMMARY: by 85% GW-54 increases love and common good to stop corruption.

Throughout our lives we long to love ourselves more deeply and to feel connected with others. Instead, we often contract, fear intimacy, and suffer a bewildering sense of separation. We crave love, and yet we are lonely. Our delusion of being separate from one another, of being apart from all that is around us, gives rise to all of this pain.

- Sharon Salzberg

Personal Field Journal Report: **Self-Awareness and Health**

WITNESS 7 Ben Chapwald
GreenWave-54 Testimony

My studies of the GreenWave-54 sensory attraction activities helped me to gain greater self-awareness and health. I feel better and relate more intelligently in general now and I'm so much more grounded than I was before I found these rare courses. They fulfill my right to education that my 19 previous years of education denied because they did not, and still do not, offer or validate GreenWave-54. Today, I know myself to be a combination of natural sensory awareness and socially conditioned reasoning in regards to what and how I have learned to know and love the world. I have identified illegitimate stories that I attach to certain situations. I understand how these stories hinder my ability to logically connect with the web and people and how to strengthen my ability to correct these stories, become more whole and help others do the same. My growth can be measured by my greater self-appreciation, adaptability, and happiness. I have placed an entire world of continual natural attractions within my psyche to, in any moment, safely unify in balance with my human, environmental, and cosmic communities. I can't teach it to my students because, unreasonably, the Department of Education does not demand it in curriculums.

WITNESS 7 SUMMARY: by 85% GW-54 heightens self-appreciation and sensory awareness.

All our knowledge begins with the senses, proceeds then to the understanding, and ends with reason. There is nothing higher than reason.
                                                                        - **Immanuel Kant**

Probable Cause Summary

Robert Goldwater, Prosecutor:

Here is my Probable Cause summary of the testimony of the sworn in witnesses to this point. From them we have learned that to maintain and to support well-being, any education is, in its methods and materials, an outgrowth of the needs of the society and the environment in which it exists.

Today, due to Earth Overshoot, all year long we personally and planet-wise, produce, register, and sense a natural resource deficiency and its effects (The State of Planet Earth and Us, 2001). We experience an emptiness or an unexplainable, discomforting void in whole life integrity in our body, mind, spirit, and the natural world. We feel out of balance and dissatisfied; things don't make sense and this conflict reduces our resilience along with the vitality of our immune system. It results from our society measurably producing an increasing deficit in Earth's environmental quality and resource capacity. It deteriorates the well-being of the environment and of humanity for we are dependent on the health of its purifying and balancing powers. This dilemma is a catastrophe in the making, the root of most of our miseries.

The destructive source and remedy for this problem is known and addressed by GreenWave-54. However, at this late date it is yet to be required, utilized, and offered by higher education, by the U.S. Department of Education, or by regional accrediting associations. This is contrary to and a breach of their published contract and responsibility to

- get information on what works in education to teachers and education policymakers for the improvement of science, mathematics, and environmental instruction;
- raise national and community awareness of the education challenges confronting the nation;
- disseminate the latest discoveries on what works in teaching and learning;
- evaluate and ensure higher education's contribution to the common good and address the needs of society and students since this is a fundamental human right to which freedom of inquiry and expression are integral; and
- help communities work out solutions to difficult educational issues by increasing student achievement and preparation for global cooperation and competitiveness, fostering educational excellence, and ensuring equal access.

In consideration of the testimony of Witness #1 with regard to Earth Overshoot and its destructive misery and other effects on human and other life forms, the Defendants have violated our constitutional rights to life, love, education, health, property and freedom of speech. It may not even be legal for them to use taxpayer money to pass judgment on what is acceptable or non-acceptable education. Who are they to decide this? Their expertise and judgment to date has educated us to be runaway excessive and create our still-increasing Earth Overshoot debt and its miseries.

 **What Earth Overshoot demonstrates** is that due to our excessiveness, for every 25-45 seconds of every minute that each of us live, some other person, place or thing of the Planet is suffering while losing their life. This reduces the quality of, or potential for, life for any person, no less any other thing or place. By omitting GreenWave-54, Higher Education allows this practice to increase each year. It lets us be socialized to reject reasonable material and emotional support directly from the life of our planet. This defies our right to love and be loved as individuals on legal, moral, and ethical grounds. By not being educated to protect the vitality of natural systems in and around us, we secretly infringe upon our freedom from torture and degrading treatment, along with the unspoken right to life of all of life. Where are these stalwarts of Education who have been given the right to teach us to continue on this track by not letting GreenWave-54 help us remedy this dilemma, no less, help them correct their own warped thinking so they may help the public do the same?

The testimony I will now present shows that GreenWave-54 (a) is privately subsidized and scientifically substantiated, (b) has been readily available for any interested party for the past 25 years, and (c) because it has a 50-year history of perfecting its function, the claims by the Plaintiffs of their civil and human rights being unnecessarily violated by the omission of GreenWave-54 by the Defendants deserve to be heard in a trial that the best thinking of this Grand Jury must sanction. The excuse that global life varies and our activities are just additional varying agents will not hold up in court. If someone severely damages your car, even if you can still drive it at risk, they are liable for the damage. If your car is then illegal to be on the road if you drive it you can be punished for breaking the law.

Carefully weigh the additional experienced witnesses and testimony that will provide you with evidence far beyond reasonable doubt about the vital contribution of GreenWave-54 and that the Defendants are guilty as charged for withholding it without cause. This is not science fiction. If you are clear thinking and not in denial, you will recognize this is already a disaster and it's increasing.

Opening Statements of Witnesses *(continued)*

Philosophical Empiricism and Scientific Evidence

WITNESS 8 Charles Bradbury
GreenWave-54 Testimony

For Justice to prevail the facts must be known and, as demonstrated by the amazing success of our human-built society and advanced technologies, the facts obtained from scientific methodology are trustable and accurate. It is self-evident that they work when applied. From a century of research about how the Universe operates and especially from the work of Albert Einstein, scientific methodology has produced the Big Bang model that was finalized in 2012. Its origin includes a singular "Higgs Boson" attraction net as Einstein's Grand Unified Field predicted. That Unified Field is the attraction core that makes up matter, including humanity as well as the origin of fundamental particles and mass. It is the "glue" the "un" in unity and unification. Its attraction energy is conscious that it is attracted to unify and bind things and relationships together, from subatomic particles to molecules to galaxies including how we think, feel and act in this moment. Attraction being conscious of what it is attracted to is the essence of love. If it was not conscious of its attraction desires Nature would not be aware of what it is attracted to and enjoy the strength of that attractive diversity. As Max Planck said, "I regard consciousness as fundamental. I regard matter as derivative from consciousness. We cannot get behind consciousness."

GreenWave-54 shows the Universe emerged from a state of extremely high temperature and density—the so-called Big Bang that occurred 13.8 billion years ago. It says that the Universe has no edge; its origin occurred not at a particular point in space but rather throughout whatever existed then at the same time. This makes it possible to calculate its sequential history of creating its attraction to creating time and space, moment-by-moment since its continual growth in this very moment as us as well as everything else. The attraction/love essence of each moment and everything in it is identical and whole life reasonable. This means that our whole Planet is an intelligent living and loving singularity (Our Living Universe, 2014).

The self-evidence used in the science of GreenWave-54 is undeniable, true, and trustable in word and deed because it almost instantly registers directly on our 54 natural senses in the moment. Our science and technology world does not need to prove it because it is felt-sense obvious that self-evidence can be gathered in the immediate moment of the Universe, that some call the "now." For example, it is self-evident that right now your sense of hearing can register my voice or your eyes can read these words of my testimony. Your attraction to do this brought you to this final word, now.

Empirical evidence based on logic is equally reasonable. For example, the logic of the number sequence from 0-9 is reasonable, and it is reasonable to accept that other members of the jury can hear my voice. Both these forms of evidence are used in scientific methodology. **Using self-evidence, GreenWave-54 validates that we have 54 natural senses, not just 5,** as well as incorporates our key missing truth of the sequential Big Bang time-space universe that Einstein predicted and the discovery of the Higgs boson "God particle" unified attraction field validated in 2012.

 **Most, if not all of the evidence used in GreenWave-54 is organic** and either self-evidence or empirical evidence. Neither is subjective. The power of GreenWave-54 is that it enables us to transform the duality that troubles us into a unified field singularity that our 54 felt-sense reasoning in the moment can tap into (Cohen, 2008). This is because these 54 senses together are the aliveness, love, consciousness and wisdom in us of the Universe's time-space, moment by moment self re-creation.

Observations of GreenWave-54 in action show that learning to think and speak while 54 sense connected to the GreenWave Dance of the Unified Field helps us communicate with the whole of life and its history as part of the attraction/love essence of our personal life in any moment. The Dance attaches us to all past and present leaders, deities, stories, senses, facts, prophecies and relationships in the history and life of Planet Earth. While we lovingly dance as 54-sense equals with them in the present, in the time between when they touch our senses and we fully process them into our awareness or stories *we can update them about our advanced science and technology progress.* In congress together this enables our natural attraction dance, moment-by-moment, to unify, transform, produce and support scientifically responsible tomorrows in peaceful balance with the whole of life, including past leaders.

WITNESS 8 SUMMARY: by 85% GW-54 strengthens our trust in scientific methodology.

> *For more than three decades, the Higgs Boson has been physicists' version of King Arthur's Holy Grail, Ponce de Leon's Fountain of Youth, Captain Ahab's Moby Dick. It's been an obsession, a fixation, an addiction to an idea that almost every expert believed just had to be true."*
> - **Stefan Soldner-Rembold**

Dynamics of Applied Psychology

WITNESS 9 Anne Barkley
GreenWave-54 Testimony:

Jurors, please do the following now. Close your eyes and imagine you are seeing the bright yellow color of a lemon wedge as you hold it.

Notice how its thick skin feels rubbery. Now bring the imaginary lemon towards your nose and with a deep breath, smell it. Place the wedge in your lips, mouth, feel your teeth against the fruit and skin. Bite into the lemon and feel your teeth as they move through the skin and the pulp. What consistency is the juice as it begins to run into your mouth? Feel it on your tongue, and on your teeth and gums. Is it cold? Warm? How does it taste? Is it sour? Is it sweet? Bitter?

Are you salivating now? You probably are; most people do. This is because our sensory 54 senses do not know the difference between what is real and what is imaginary until, in concert, our senses of consciousness and reason assess the experience.

Other than humanity, no animal, plant, mineral or energy is literate. They do not understand stories we write or tell. Everything we have ever sensed with our bodies is stored in our mentality. When a story about one of your senses brings to mind some sensory reality, your mind, body and spirit tends to react as if the sensory stimulus were really there. In the Big Bang Universe, the ramifications of this phenomenon are far reaching when a story is inaccurate for it becomes a habitual or fixed, addictive way of thinking that is difficult to unravel or correct its effects (Cohen, 1993).

> *In the beginning was the word and the word was "distortion" or "corrupt" because the beginning was not a word.*
>
> - **God** <grin>

> *If you wish to make an apple pie from scratch, you must first invent the universe.*
>
> - **Carl Sagan**

A thriller movie, or threatening statement, or description of a sad event can make you feel and respond like it was real yet each of them is imaginary. Any information that that you think is true makes this happen. In addition, our body protectively hides the discomfort of being wrong, stressed, or hurt by storing these feelings in our subconscious mind. There they subconsciously stress us as our daily lives threaten to hook them into feeling their discomfort. This fear influences and often warps how we think, feel, and act. It is a source of corruption (Cohen, 2007a).

 A person that never knew what a lemon was or never experienced one would not salivate when I read the lemon instructions. They would be unprepared to know what to expect from a lemon, good or bad. That is the value of the First Amendment, the right to free speech. It enables our stories to acquaint us with all that is known or imagined so that our reasoning can be more reasonable and our lives more sensible.

I am giving each of you a list that GreenWave-54 uses *(see Appendix, page 82, Ed.)*. It names the scientifically validated 54 senses that most normal people are born with to help them register the world correctly and rationally felt—sense, think, and relate in balance with Nature (PNC, 1997). You can use it as a checklist in considering the testimony of the witnesses. Notice that in addition to our 5 senses it includes our sense groups of temperature, color, reason, pressure, gravity, consciousness, excretion, space, motion, literacy, chemicals, pain, love, humor, place, thirst, humility, fear, time, aliveness, distress, and trust. In the moments when you have experienced and processed them they were undeniable, self-evident facts of your life.

The major difference between the rest of nature and us on planet Earth is that we alone create and relate through stories that can be accurate for our life in balance or that can mislead and hurt us. Until we can tell the difference and, in addition, know how to reasonably select accurate stories for Nature and ourselves, we are fooled into habitually or addictively living in ways that hurt Earth's and our web-of-life as shown by Earth Overshoot (PNC, 2001). GreenWave-54 only uses the most accurate stories produced by scientific methodology to provide us with an important safeguard and remedy for this destructive phenomenon (Cohen, 2009). The GreenWave-54 story is to develop stories that create moments in natural areas that let the life of Earth teach us what we need to know in its/our non-story, 54 sense way. Then we can know and speak reasonable stories from what our 54 senses register in those moments (Cohen, 2007b). This is of major importance because, as shown in behavioral epigenetics, this phenomenon not only affects how our genetics express themselves but it carries over to our descendants, too (Alban, 2016). Scientifically GreenWave-54 is faith in action.

WITNESS 9 SUMMARY: by 85% GW-54 strengthens whole life equality.

The kind of education science offers teaches us to be neglectful of nothing—not to despise the small beginnings, for they precede of necessity all great things in the knowledge of science, either pure or applied.
- **Michael Faraday, 1857**

Personal Field Journal Report: **Nature's Pain Reliever**.

WITNESS 10 William Barlow
GreenWave-54 Testimony:

When I was doing this activity in the natural area on campus, I started to shuffle my feet through the dried leaves. I suddenly realized that my pain had stopped and I concentrated on the very pleasant sound of the dried leaves under my feet. I stopped walking through the leaves and slowly the pain returned, so I started walking again and sure enough the pain resolved again. I thought, this natural love is Nature's pain reliever. The sound of the leaves and my steps added energy to it. My rights to be free of pain, torture, and degrading treatment are being infringed upon by the absence of GreenWave-54 in this school.

WITNESS 10 SUMMARY: by 85% GW-54 enhances pain reduction.

Love is the only sane and satisfactory answer to the problem of human existence.

- **Erich Fromm**

Unified Field Attraction and Applied Logic

WITNESS 11 Roger Young
GreenWave-54 Testimony:

Natural attraction or attractiveness can be defined as the act, process, or power of attracting or loving to bring about a unifying response. Natural attraction is the Higgs Boson unifying force acting mutually between particles of matter, energy, or life relationships. It tends to draw them together and resists their separation. When you sense that you want to survive, that feeling is the universal attraction love to live expressing itself in and as you.

To date no provable deviation has been found to the core principle of GreenWave-54, that moment-by-moment all things in the Universe are simultaneously in a self-promoting and self-organizing natural attraction-based relationship with each other as well as with the dance of the whole Big Bang universe as it creates its own time and space. This is because GreenWave-54 includes John Muir's fundamental ecology principle of connectedness: *When we try to pick out anything by itself we find that it is bound fast by a thousand invisible cords that cannot be broken (are attracted/attached) to everything in the universe.*

Albert Einstein observed that the Universe is attracted to expanding as a vibrating, immediate moment, unified field of time and space attraction that GreenWave-54 calls the "Dance of the Universe and its Aliveness". Every part of it is an attractive dancer that is consciously connected, attracted, or attached to other dancers as attraction/loves of the Grand Unified Field. This makes repulsion to, in reality, be a form of attraction to greater attractiveness. Similarly, when in we are in danger we run or fight *for* our life because it is attractive.

Scientifically, the Higgs boson "God particle" is an original Big Bang attraction energy that produces the unified attraction field of the Universe, as Einstein predicted (Green, 2013). *GreenWave-54 is the unified field and its evidence-based history.*

The Universe and its conscious unified field, life, love and grace are synonymous names for natural attraction. They are found everywhere, including in or as "God" when God is unconditional love that includes the total web-of-life.

> *For what else is Nature but God and the Divine Reason that pervades the whole universe and all its parts.*
>
> **- Seneca the Younger** 25 A.D

This is also observed in scripture:

God is love. Whoever lives in love lives in God, and God in them."
                                                    - **John 4:16** Revised Standard Version

Jesus said:
*I am the light that is above them all. I am the all; the all came forth from me,
and the all attained to me. Cleave a piece of wood; I am there. Raise up a stone,
and you will find me there.*
                                                    - **Gospel of Thomas** [77]

Be it God or not, humans possess an innate attraction to seek connections with nature and other forms of life, a passionate love of life/survival and of all that is alive that some scientists called Biophilia. What George Lucas really meant in Star Wars is "May the ~~force~~ *love* be with you."

Repulsion between dancers in the Dance of the Universe does not exist. It is a misinterpretation of the Dance because the Dance is solely a singular, vibrant and resonating sway of attractions to more attractive dances, dancers and aliveness. I repeat, things are not repulsed into surviving, rather they run for their life, for greater attraction relationships and the life support they provide. For example, magnets only repel each other when our stories or some other force manipulate their poles to do so. In their natural state their dance is to attract each other. This is equally true of atomic relationships that our stories can manipulate into becoming nuclear bombs

Since the essence of the Universe is its attraction to produce and sustain the life of its unifying attraction field in each moment, it can't have repulsions. Rather it has greater or weaker attractions. This means fear, pain and depression are natural attraction signals to beneficially find and fulfill new or greater attractions. It explains why the life of Nature produces no garbage or negatives. In any moment all things are attracted to each other and belong. It is our nature-disconnected or conquering stories that produce and are Nature negatives. Since Nature only works with attractions, it is vulnerable to these imagined negatives that our stories convey.

Because Nature happens all at once continually, humanity's stories invented "time" so that we have space to sense, think, feel and act attractively via stories. However, this behavior only takes place in the now so as we produce our stories they influence the present. It's like we put a camera in a flowing river and it changes the river flow... then the camera photographs the river's behavior at that moment and we say that is how nature works, not how it works without our camera or story intruding. When we can't substantiate these stories we create new mystical stories to explain them. The latter mislead us to produce many problems including earth misery. When we CRL surf the crest of the GreenWave we avoid or correct this blunder because we are conscious that we are in the now and that we are creating or fixing stories with the wisdom of the GreenWave.

Our awareness registers Nature through the warp of our screen of consciousness. It can look like competition not cooperation, repulsion rather belonging, sin rather than collaboration, danger rather than support. GreenWave experiences including the perceptions of other folks that are present help us rectify this phenomenon.

Our bias omits that the Na'vi and Pandora in James Cameron's Avatar are GreenWave-54 humanity and Earth without our nature-disconnecting stories and Steven Spielberg neglects to mention that ET is Earth, not an extraterrestrial.

Science works because consistently, like the 0-9 logical sequence of numerals, or like a plant growing from its seed, **everything is seamlessly attracted/attached to all that has gone before it and remains attached to all that follows it into the next moment.** This reflects the sequential time/space process and continuum of the Big Bang Universe. It makes it accessible in any given moment. Mathematics simply symbolizes it into numbers.

The dancers that we are and we call Humanity inherently have 54 natural attraction senses whose sensations are natural attraction facts and intelligence. For example, thirst is our attraction for water; trust is our attraction for safe support. Each different sense and sensation is a form of love for life, a motivation for fulfillment and the happiness it produces as it supports life. The senses' unifying powers, in concert and with enthusiasm, reasonably register, guide, balance, and heal relationships. For example, thirst is intelligent and self-fulfilling enough to know when to bring the global water cycle in and through us, while excretion knows when to remove soiled water from us and feed the Planet with it, thus purifying the water. Note that thirst, excretion, and trust are not included in the 5 senses we are taught that we have. However, they are included in GreenWave-54 as are our love of consciousness, reason, and literacy. We often overlook that love is conscious of itself. It also includes the means for us to think and feel with our 54 senses habitually.

WITNESS 11 SUMMARY: by 85% GW-54 reduces fear, negativity and depression.

For small creatures such as we, the vastness is bearable only through love.
— **Carl Sagan**

Personal Field Journal Report: **Nature's Power and Beauty**

WITNESS 12 Gene Bellvue
GreenWave-54 Testimony:

    The GreenWave-54 courses gave me a previously missing respect for my actions and a feeling of dignity, that I had the Right to Love and Be loved: I aligned myself with my natural surroundings, letting their energy fill me, while remaining flexible enough to allow it to pass through me without conflict. Aligning and drawing in the attraction energy from various elements of the natural environment increases balance and harmony. When I have feelings of anxiety, I can reasonably connect to the web of life and it is attracted to embrace me with comfort, guidance and wisdom that I have been missing. I get the feeling of being "one" with its power and beauty and GreenWave-54 gave this ability to most folks in the courses I took.

I was especially taken by the program's ability to help me to discover that our Universe consists of natural attraction that is conscious of its attraction to increase its attractiveness. My 54 senses experienced this as planet Earth, around, in and as me, moment-by-moment becoming more diverse attraction relationships. I think of it as "Nature is love extending its love to be more loving."

My interactions with many students has had a very positive impact on all of them. They now look at nature in a different way and feel very much connected to it. Their social lives have certainly improved as they are breaking their fear of nature and instead embrace it. Some have had life changing experiences.

WITNESS 12 SUMMARY: by 85% GW-54 intensifies harmony and our rights to life and love.

> *There is no remedy for love but to love more.*
>   **- Henry David Thoreau**

> *The natural world is the larger sacred community to which we belong. To be alienated from this community is to become destitute in all that makes us human. To damage this community is to diminish our own existence.*
>   **- Thomas Berry**

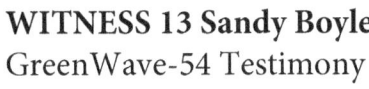

Cosmology and Behavioral Physics

WITNESS 13 Sandy Boyle
GreenWave-54 Testimony

Because it has built itself since its beginning, at any given moment the Big Bang Universe is a singular unified attraction/love energy dance that creates the "now" time and space of the Universe and the next moment of itself that it builds. We learn to overlook that this means whenever we know we are alive and this is reasonable, the whole Universe and all parts of it are this aliveness because the two are identical. This aliveness consists of attraction/love that becomes energy, atoms, our senses, our Planet, the stars, and galaxies. It explains why rocks, stars, and galaxies are observed to have slow but measurable life cycles.

At this late date the reason the scientific process still cannot distinguish between life and death is because the essence of everything is alive, all things are attracted to live and love to stay alive in our living Planet and Universe. The aliveness of the Big Bang can be seen as an originating cosmic orgasm that gave birth to the life of our Universe and continues to do so, moment-by-moment. As might be expected, many forms of life, including human life, display this process because they are it.

Natural attraction is alive and produces different forms of its aliveness, moment by moment. The aliveness part of us today was there in the Big Bang then and is a seamless continuum of that love to live now. Our 54 natural senses along with the Unified Field are attractive Big Bang aliveness in action (Our living universe, 2014).

The purpose of life is to support life because life/survival is attractive. Life consciously loves to live. Death is a reasonable attraction to transform into a stronger form of attractive aliveness. For this reason, Nature produces no garbage. Everything, including humanity, is attractive, alive, belongs, and cooperatively contributes to the welfare of the whole of life since the beginning of time and space.

Humanity lives in, not on, our Living Planet Earth/Gaia, deep under its atmosphere and in its biosphere. We are each a uniquely evolved personification of Earth's loving alive, metabolism.. The resources and ways of Mother Earth are our placenta to the life of the Universe. A placenta is alive.

WITNESS 13 SUMMARY: by 85% GW-54 supports personal and global aliveness.

The whole universe in its different spans and wave-lengths, exclusions and developments, is everywhere alive and conscious. There is one fundamental stuff.
                                                                    - **William James**, 1887

Personal Field Journal Report: **We are Truly One**

WITNESS 14 Janet Whelm
GreenWave-54 Testimony

I just walked outside, and started walking along the waterfront, connecting with various beings of nature a person-size bush with yellow blooming flowers, a tree with bulbs that looked like they are getting ready to open; weeds, thorns, grass, sun, air, and water. The bush was the first one I connected with, repeating "unity" in my mind. The reaction was almost immediate, and I had a sense/vision much like the ending of The Matrix, when Neo sees everything like flowing energy, himself included. I was in a different country, one that protected me from being injured by the hostile lack of unity that I endure when I'm at home or school. I felt very similar, in a deep and visceral way being one with the bush. There was simply difference in our physical form, yet we were built out of the same "thing" pure energy or love. It continued with all other beings I encountered along the way back home. I had to slow down, walk slowly and mindfully, and maintain the focus on this experience.

I could feel that we are truly are all one, that I was fulfilling my right to seek asylum if a country treats me badly. In this protective GreenWave-54 country the underlying energy in all being is very much the same, and can be tapped into almost immediately once the intention is present. I recognize that GreenWave-54 helps me get good feelings from being near water, from feeling the sun on my being, and from allowing my senses to wander around, without any specific and particular focus. I love the GreenWave with all my heart because it is my heart.

WITNESS 14 SUMMARY: by 85% GW-54 strengthens the sense and vision of unity

If you watch how nature deals with adversity, continually renewing itself, you can't help but learn.

- Bernie Seigel, M.D.

Universal and Living Planet Consciousness

WITNESS 15 Robert Brown
GreenWave-54 Testimony

In our Planet and Universe, everything contains an intelligent consciousness. To create and sustain the astounding dance of life, Earth's natural attraction essence must be intelligent enough to achieve this.

Nature's life-dance within and around us consists of conscious, wild, attraction-based, optimums that become stronger and more attractive through cooperating diversity. The dance accomplishes this by being aware of and following its attractions rather than disregarding or omitting their signals. This is reasonable.

Natural attraction is both motivation and intelligent awareness in action. It is conscious that it is attracted to self-correcting life, love, diversity, balance, fairness, cooperation, sanity, and purity. Nature does not create excessiveness, greed, garbage, stress, corruption, depression, madness, abusiveness, dependencies, or conflicting stories because they are not attractive. Any person or thing that can make this happen would have to be considered intelligent (Magic of Something from Nothing, 2012).

Any moment in human consciousness consists of either Nature-disconnected stories or 54 attraction-connected thoughts, sensations, feelings, and stories.

The fittest survive in Organism Earth because they are the most intelligent builders of attractive, cooperative, mutually beneficial relationships that support the Planet's life dance. They also help other species help them be fit by strengthening their cooperative relationships with them. This makes reasonable the wisdom of the ages be that natural attraction love is the only truth.

With respect to survival, the intelligence of natural attraction can be seen in the slime mold. As reported in *Scientific American* "Compared with most organisms, slime molds have been on the planet for a very long time—they first evolved at least 600 million years ago and perhaps as long as one billion years ago. At the time, no organisms had yet evolved brains or even simple nervous systems. Yet slime molds do not blindly ooze from one place to another—they carefully explore their environments, seeking the most efficient routes between resources. They can solve mazes. They do not accept whatever circumstances they find themselves in, but rather choose conditions most amenable to their survival. They remember, anticipate and decide. By doing **so much with so little,** slime molds represent a successful and admirable alternative to convoluted brain-based intelligence. (Cohen, 2012)"

The Slime Mold consists of a more than 13 billion year sequence of the preceding life of the Universe being attracted to manifesting its life sensibly from moment one on. In the art and science of Educating, Counseling and Healing With Nature (ECHN) this is doing "a lot with a whole lot". It is not "so little" as the objective bias of a "convoluted brain science story" reports in *Scientific American.*

The Slime Mold's attraction process in the maze is the essence of how scientists and science are attracted to work. "Gather all the evidence/information and eliminate that which does not bring you to your reasonable goal." This achieves the pure and balanced whole life results that we desperately need today because it includes all the evidence available.

The Slime Mold has many of, or more than our 53 sense (no story-telling literacy) consciousness of our and its origins in Nature. As does all reasonable science, the mold identifies its whole situation, including "subjective information." It then follows its many natural sensory attractions to discover and gather as much knowledge as is possible with regard to its singular sensory/attraction/hunger for food, or other necessities such as temperature and moisture.

Once the Mold finds the food, it bypasses or dries up the false routes it discovered in the process. This indicates that the Mold makes reasonable, self-evident, multisensory, singularity sense from: "food or no-food," or "something or nothing." That is the same as the workings of a computer  or mathematics "one or zero", *or* the Big Bang of the Universe "Higgs Boson Attraction Universe *or* some other Universe." The process enables the mold to follow the accurate and reasonably attractive sensory route sequence that leads to the food as well as obtain rewarding attraction and survival fulfillments for doing so.

Unlike the Mold and to our loss, our material-based Objective Science omits most of our 54 natural attraction senses, like hunger, calling them "subjective" or "phenomenological evidence" or some belief system name. It ignores their callings and instead applauds itself for stories that help people invent dynamite to blow open holes in the Maze's walls to obtain life-supportive fulfillment from not only food but salaries, funding, social power and public acclaim as being first class "effective dynamiters" be they football players, engineers or politicians.

As exemplified by the sensation of thirst, on cellular and molecular levels, sensors (senses and their sensations) in an organism, large(Earth) or small(nanobe), are receptors that are attracted to detect stimuli. When the information that they register is out of balance, they become the *main homeostatic driving force* for change that promotes life in balance. Their detection process is a fundamental source that functions on mechanical, thermal and chemical levels as it promotes the survival of life. When they are not adulterated by nature-disconnecting stories the senses can be depended on as self-evident, recovery and balancing tools that are part of every space/time moment. Whatever any of our 54 senses find attractive in nature is what is doing the finding.

 Everything in the web of life, including the Slime Mold relates through the same reasonable, immediate life of Earth intelligence as do some human societies. The latter know how to consciously 54-sense connect with it and have not produced our problems.

Mathematics puts into symbols the unified field events that take place in the progression of the Universe that produce signals in the form of waves traveling through space time. When these waves collapse on the human senses they are transferred to the brain, which homeostatically processes them and modulates them to perceptible sensory formats such as colors, sounds, tastes, etc., If such information is reprocessed to establish relationships between previous outputs from the brain, any established relationships stored in memory become mathematical formulations that reflect some aspect of physical reality from a human perspective. It therefore follows that mathematics is not invented, it is a story reflection of natural *survival attraction* signals that are input and subsequently modulated by the human mind into symbol images and their story.

Simply stated, as earlier, the logical beginning and continuing sequence of the **GreenWave *non-story* Universe** and the ***abstract symbol story*** sequence of mathematic numerals is identical. This explains why math, when not adulterated, is the essence of accurate story thinking and information in our science based society.

Being indoctrinated to self-deprive from over 50 "subjective" natural attraction senses, the desensitized prejudice of scientific objectivity and thinking has yet to acknowledge that the whole maze for the Slime Mold is the life of Planet Earth. Out of shame our conscious thinking ignores that our "objectivity" is unreasonably and unfairly blasting holes in the maze that violate human, civil and constitutional rights while producing our destructive imbalances.

WITNESS 15 SUMMARY: by 85% GW-54 increases intelligent attraction consciousness.

> *Truth is by nature self-evident. As soon as you remove the cobwebs of ignorance that surround it, it shines clear.*
> - Mahatma Gandhi

Personal Field Journal Report: **Safely Unify in Balance**

WITNESS 16 Susan Aaron
GreenWave-54 Testimony

I am a person who feels great when I take the time to shut off the inner chatter and explore nature with many senses. When I do so, I feel that I am part of a huge organism called earth, and that I share in the collective wisdom and strength of Earth. These activities that I have been doing are deceptively simple: they are powerful and healing. (I spend time in nature, I immerse myself in it, what difference could a few simple words or particular approach make……………..all the difference in the world………yes, deceptively simple….amazingly effective!)

GreenWave-54 helps me to gain greater self-awareness and health. I feel better and relate more intelligently in general now, I have strengthened my right to life, liberty, and personal security. I know myself to be a combination of natural sensory awareness and socially conditioned reasoning in regards to what and how I have learned to know the world. I have identified stories that I attach to certain situations, how these stories limit my freedom to use my ability to logically connect with the web and people and how to strengthen my ability to correct these stories and become more whole. My growth can be measured by my greater self-appreciation, adaptability, and happiness. By using GreenWave-54 I have placed an entire world of continual natural attractions within my psyche to, in any moment, safely unify in balance with my human, environmental, and cosmic communities (Thinking and Learning Our Living Universe, 2011).

WITNESS 16 SUMMARY: by 85% GW-54 restores the wisdom of reasonable happiness.

For the things we have to learn before we can do, we learn by doing.
- Aristotle

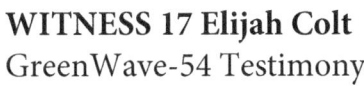

The Lie of Omission

WITNESS 17 Elijah Colt
GreenWave-54 Testimony

Here are a few quotes from the past 2500 years that show that the information I believe must have been presented by witnesses today has long been available and known. The negligence of the Defendants denies people's right to it by avoiding or omitting it by not including GreenWave-54 in Higher Education. As noted by Baruch Spinoza in 1661: *Nature offers nothing that can be called this man's rather than another's; but under nature everything belongs to all—that is, they have authority to claim it for themselves.*

The Universe is a single living creature that encompasses all living creatures within it.
　　　- Plato, 420 BC

The Tao is the sustaining Life-force and the mother of all things; from it, all things rise and fall without cease.
　　　- Tao Te Ching, 600 BC

We followers of Spinoza see our God in the wonderful order and lawfulness of all that exists and in its soul as it reveals itself in man and animal. Time and space and gravitation have no separate existence from matter.
　　　- Albert Einstein, 1935

And because we are alive, the universe must be said to be alive. We are its consciousness as well as our own. We rise out of the cosmos and we see its mesh of patterns, and it strikes us as beautiful. And that feeling is the most important thing in the entire universe—its culmination, like the color of the flower at first bloom on a wet morning.
　　　- Kim Stanley Robinson, 1935

WITNESS 17 SUMMARY: by 85% GW-54 affirms our right to demand whole life facts anywhere

We are more likely to destroy ourselves with our persistent and worldwide conflict with nature than in any war with weapons ever devised.
　　　- Fairfield Osborne, 1948

Hard Science Social Relationships

WITNESS 18 Elise Whitney
GreenWave-54 Testimony

The scientific discovery of Nature's Higgs Boson attraction-based birth of the life of our Universe is the essence of our social relationships as well as all other natural relationships. Converging scientific evidence shows that we only exist in the attraction-based sequence of time and space "now" moments of the Universe that we call its Unified Field. The past and future only exist as their influence on the Unified Field of the present moment.

As humans we live either in immediate attraction relationships via our 54 natural attraction senses or in our stories, be they scientifically accurate or not. Building relationships based on our inaccurate stories produces problems. Our unreasonable stories can't solve them when our senses are attached or addicted to them so they addictively govern our behavior.

Our story world most reasonably and accurately transmits how nature works through mathematics whose 0-9 number sequence accurately symbolizes the flawless sequence of the Unified Field. However, the use of Mathematics is limited in relating to the Unified Field because

The number one does not exist in Nature except in any single moment since all of nature is dancing, flowing, and changing moment by moment. Because there are no standard conditions in Nature, identifying "one" is not possible over time or in general.

The number zero does not exist in nature since GreenWave-54 attraction bonds between things exist everywhere. Nowhere is there nothing in Nature. This means that objective science is based on mathematics that don't apply to Nature's unified field.

Objective science and technology are destructively runaway because in any given moment their limits make our thinking omit the in-the-moment guiding energy and subjective sensory facts of our 53 natural attraction senses. Whenever objective reasoning omits the totality of our 54 natural sensibilities it is unreasonable with respect to the welfare of the whole of life.

Relationships can stop being runaway and come into organic balance by reasonably including our 54 natural senses as objective science, genuine, self-evident facts of life. That lets scientific thinking help us relate to the unified field through the 54-sense whole life aliveness of our Planet. This self-governs and corrects people, places and things in a unified way.

GreenWave-54 works because learning to think and speak while connected to the attraction Dance of the Unified Field in any given moment helps us lovingly communicate with the non-storied whole of life and its eons of history. That enables us to practice whole life science.

As we dance as 54-sense equals with the past in the Unified Field present, we unite with and can update the past with today's advanced knowledge. We can walk with Jesus or anybody else in a natural area and *help these great folks bring their science and technology skills up to date.* Until then, it is like getting advice for today's life from fools. Dancing the Dance with them updated enables our stories and senses to increase well-being as our disorders transform into responsible, new Unified Field moments in peaceful balance with the whole of life now. This process transitions our nature disconnection into additional whole-life integrity. To not use it is like trying to stop our car horse and buggy style, by pulling on the steering wheel while yelling, "whoa" as we crash further into Earth overshoot misery.

GreenWave-54 empowers our thinking to reasonably fill our lives with the balance, beauty and wellness afforded by our attractive 54 Unified Field connections in natural areas. Today there is no responsible substitute for this since we are already out of balance. It lets Nature happily unify and heal us because that's how Nature works. To withhold it invites disaster.

WITNESS 18 SUMMARY: by 85% GW-54 sustains us lovingly communicating with the eons.

I don't understand why when we destroy something created by man we call it vandalism, but when we destroy something created by nature we call it progress.
- **Ed Begley, Jr**.

Personal Field Journal Report: **Freedom of Belief and Religion**

WITNESS 19 Larry Singleton
GreenWave-54 Testimony:

These exercises have been cathartic because to stop and reflect upon the more rewarding natural encounters was not only enjoyable but reflection upon them fed me in many unimaginable ways. Since returning to the larger United States, I have systematically grown further and further from the spectacular rawness of the rain forest. I have fought this disconnect daily, but now I have a daughter who has not been raised in the same nature-oriented manner that I was. This poses a dilemma for me. Being able to consciously connect to nature as a GreenWave-54 spirituality or religion that mimics the scientific approach towards non-literate relationships is affording me personal rejuvenation, a safe method or place to share my unique background and will allow me to bridge the nature gap between my daughter's upbringing and my own. In this way GreenWave-54 stops my Freedom of Belief and Religion from being unreasonably eroded by my return to the United States (Peak Fact, 2010).

The application of GreenWave-54 on a wide scale could have major ramifications on the future of our planet. By using the process and learning to perceive nature in a more communicative mode, the individual receives numerous gifts, which include the ability to receive/hear one's own truth, to achieve a strong level of peace and balance, to recover from disorders and to honor the environment. These gifts, if consistently appreciated and acted upon, would lead to less dependency on chemical substances, less conflict, less stress, less disorders, less resource use, less war, less environmental desecration. The world could achieve through the Einstein's unified field a loving state of balance that is the natural rhythm found in nature.

Without us using GreenWave-54 our increasingly destructive frustrations due to our Nature-separated emotional deprivation reminds me of the most ferocious animal in the world, the Tiglion. On one end it is the head of a lion, the other end the head of a tiger. It's so ferocious because it can't defecate.

WITNESS 19 SUMMARY: by 85% GW-54 reinforces our safe personal rejuvenation.

A scientist lives with all reality. There is nothing better. To know reality is to accept it, and eventually to love it.
                                                            - George Wald

The Philosophy of Critical Thinking

WITNESS 20 Mary Fisher
GreenWave-54 Testimony

Critical thinking is a core part of the hard science methodology that has produced our present lifestyle advantages and our technological advances. In considering the testimony no doubt presented here as well as the workings of GreenWave-54 I find that the only exception to all the information that will be given to this jury is a few scientifically inaccurate, nature-disconnected or mystical stories that deny the importance or rationale of GreenWave-54. The true story is that the Unified Field essence of our Universe is living, self-correcting, organic wellness and so is every part of it including Earth and our 54 senses. The only exception to this is our unscientific stories. They disconnect the sensibility of our 54 senses from the Field and its organic well-being. When we disconnect from it we lose its whole life wellness and produce our disorders. When we reconnect, we gain organic wellness and whole life resilience. This phenomenon becomes self-evident when we spend some quiet time in a natural area. Our stress reduces and we feel revitalized. However, our habitual nature-disconnected stories warp our thinking by explaining this organic normalcy of the Unified Field as "An escape from real-life and our problems." Really? The organic life of the Field, Nature and Earth is fake life? How much more wrong could we be? To explain this disastrous error with mystical stories just makes it harder to correct it.

A study published in Skeptical Inquirer magazine in 2006 showed that college seniors and grad students were more likely than freshmen to believe in non-evidence based things such as psychics, telepathy and channeling, reincarnation, the "evil eye," astrology, communication with the dead, haunted houses and ghostly encounters.

Contemporary people, on average, spend over 99% of their time engaged in felt-sense thinking and feeling that is neither in tune with or makes conscious sensory contact with Nature. We are using only 15 % of our total ability to make sense by using GreenWave-54 attraction/love evidence and this has produced our "unsolvable" Earth Overshoot deficit and its misery factors that violate civil and human rights.

Our unscientific or metaphysical or mystical stories may be true in some other, presently unknown or imaginary universe. However, they are invalid in building our relationships on Earth until they become validated through scientific methodology. This is because when it is reasonably combined with 54-sense evidence its objectivity helps us felt-sense think and relate like the balanced, self-correcting life of the Big Bang universe of our Planet works, while it also helps us send folks to the moon and back if it makes sense to do so. This combination enables us to think in the consensus of 54 con-senses when we practice whole-life art and science.

In physics the non-language world of nature's matter, space, time, and energy are locked (grokked) together in the most intimate embrace of the moment. In Organic Psychology we enjoy that wonderful hug because in a natural area our GreenWave story helps our 54 natural senses grok it and share it with each other, including verbally.

Time does not exist in Nature, Nature is time. To stop to even consider a moment is our story disconnect from what Nature actually does, that being non-stop. In Nature, we live in and act out our stories so what we think, feel and act become a function of Nature in that moment. It's like we put a camera in a flowing river and it changes the river flow, then, the camera photographs the river's behavior at that moment and we say that is how nature works, not how it works without our camera or story intruding.

By adding our 54 ECHN natural attraction senses to the accuracy of Objective Science, its destructively runaway powers enlist Earth's self-organizing and purifying abilities to produce balance, healing, and peace instead of our present deficiencies in resources, reasonableness and well-being (Who, What or When is the Acronym NNIAAL?, 2013).

The purpose of GreenWave-54 is to offer guaranteed methods and materials that help people create moments that let Organism Earth/Gaia teach us what we need to know. The agencies responsible for making this possible have neglected doing this for 25 years. Their negligence violates the rights of a wide range of citizens and they are liable for their irresponsibility causing a wide range of damage to many aspects of people, places, and things. Critical thinking makes it evident that this is little different than a terrorist attack on our people and our land by destructive ideas. Having not protected us from this assault, the Defense Department could also legally be defendants here.

WITNESS 20 SUMMARY: by 85% GW-54 invigorates organically based critical thinking.

The whole of science is nothing more than a refinement of everyday thinking.
— **Albert Einstein**

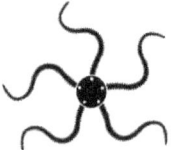

Personal Field Journal Report: **Survival and Healing**

WITNESS 21 Peter Strand
GreenWave-54 Testimony

I went to a small field near where I work. It has some brown grasses, large weeds and a few small trees and some large bushes. Most people would not consider that area attractive or me attractive for being attracted to it. I have recently been in significant discomfort due to some of my illnesses and when I started my activity my feeling of being seen as strange made me uncertain if I could connect with any attraction there.

I immediately received a strong and positive connection that validated my right to privacy. My first attraction was to my sense of emotional place. I felt immediately as if the plants and nature in general not only gave me permission to connect but strongly wanted me to connect due to my current discomfort. I had a feeling of healing and nurturing emanating from all life forms, including a thin vine of poison ivy. I also noticed my aesthetic sense, as I noted how the weeds and grasses, struggled to grow in the fields cluttered my man made litter. Trees and bushes even after having been hacked on and mutilated by mankind still continued to bud and flourish. These two connections strengthened my sense of survival and healing as I felt nature pouring its wisdom and healing ways into me.

WITNESS 21 SUMMARY: by 85% GW-54 supports my healing attraction to emotional place.

The interior landscape responds to the character and subtlety of the exterior landscape; the shape of the individual mind is affected by the land as it is by genes.

- Barry Lopez

Fundamentals of GreenWave-54

WITNESS 22 Michael J. Cohen
GreenWave-54 Testimony

As the founder of Greenwave-54, my testimony here verifies the excellence of the witnesses and the information being presented to this Grand Jury, and that I have been of assistance in assuring its and their quality. I, along with many others, have personally experienced the facts of GreenWave-54 and we hold its truths to be self-evident. They demonstrate that the stories contemporary people attach to and live by omit 85 percent of the natural attraction sensibilities that our inherent sensory connections to Nature's unified field offer us. It is this wisdom that the life of Earth lives by to produce and enjoy its perfection. I learned this as I researched and developed GreenWave-54 at Project NatureConnect for over fifty-five years (Doherty, 2010; Cohen 1993).

Motivated by my elementary school's unjust and emotionally hurtful discipline to change my six-year old's left-handed nature to right-handedness in 1936, I have dedicated my life to using the art and science of Education and Counseling with Nature to protect Nature from harm, in and around others and myself.

Because my extended family assured me that it was perfectly fine for my nature to be left-handed I have over the decades been able to accurately identify and address the point source of our runaway problems. We indoctrinate ourselves to be in denial. We deny that we are at war with Nature because our half-truth scientific stories that we emotionally attach to don't acknowledge that we have 54 natural senses, even while we experience them, one of them being our "handedness". If we can't trust the unadulterated truth of our experience, then what can we trust? Our limited-sense stories disconnect our sense of reason from the life of our planet home while it loves to sustain our lives moment by moment. This is why when we injure the life of Earth we injure the integrity and foundation of our lives. Until we correct our stories' foundation we can't stop our lies and corruption.

In developing the GreenWave-54 process I have achieved several Master's and Doctoral degrees (Cohen, 2008), written 11 books, directed environmental education and outdoor education accredited courses and degree programs for over 50 years as well as helped develop and and lived in many year-long "utopian community" expeditions. I have been recognized as a Maverick Genius, received the Distinguished World Citizen award and experientially "solved" Albert Einstein's Unified Field

Equation (Cohen 2013). I warrant the accuracy of my work and guarantee its quality because it is based on empirical evidence (Maverick Genius at Work, 2015, Impossible Dream, 2011-2013). If I could find the support that I need for it I could design an "application" that helped anybody master GreenWave-54, especially if it was required for graduation, to vote, be a leader, a protestor or in the armed forces. It would help transform nature-disconnected stories into GreenWave-54 whole life science.

This all may sound extreme but so is the situation. Our salvation is that any person who knows that part of them loves nature is eligible to train that part to become a GreenWave-54 joy, livelihood or hobby, and help others do the same.

In 1965, a transformational experience in the Grand Canyon scientifically convinced me that Earth acted in homeostatic ways, like any living organism, and that acts of nature and humanity must be scientifically explained from this point of view (Cohen, 2010). This led me to found and create the process of Expedition Education and the 1985 National Audubon Society International Symposium "Is the Earth a Living Organism." I hoped its outcome would verify "Organism Earth" that could then be protected under the Endangered Species Act as the only one of its kind. What I learned the hard way was that information alone changes very little with respect to habitual thinking and behavior.

I have established that by applying the sensory science of GreenWave-54, human beings can enjoy part or all of themselves as being a unique personification of the Unified Field life dance of the Universe and its manifestation of itself as Organism Earth or Gaia. Each of its web-of-life dancer's attractions to live are violated by contemporary humanity's nature-disconnected stories. This is because they block the Dance's flow of love and that deteriorates the Dance, in and around us.

By dancing with others on the GreenWave in natural areas for most of my life I have become it. My stories have reasonably learned to let my 54 sensibilities experience my life and everything else as the love of the Universe to live its life with me as part of it.

> I sense and feel how that love self-organized itself. It loved itself into being its dance and it started with its Big Bang "orgasm."
>
> That love at that time, and moment-by-moment since then, grew and grows lovelier. It accomplishes this by loving to love Nature/Earth more diversely around and in me. That continuously makes it a greater, stronger love, an

attraction that loves to support its love of life as well as unified field love. For example, a blackberry bush only needs one seed in one berry to replenish itself. The remainder of its berries are food that supports life of all kinds of blackberry eaters. In turn, their love of life does the same for the lives they support. As if demented, our hard science story calls this love process "competition."

GreenWave-54 is an organic technology of behavior that enables us to *grok* the essence of love because it is it. To grok means to understand and empathize with something or someone to the point that the object or person becomes part of our sense of self and we exist in its embodiment. Like a cell of an organism.

GreenWave-54 is who I've consciously become. It is also what I do and teach. When I will myself to grok a natural area, my 54 senses register and build relationships with quantum love. Anybody can learn to do this, especially if they already respect or love nature.

My life consists of making playgrounds for my way of life. Sometimes this is inconvenient for non-GreenWave folks. It makes me seem like I'm stubborn or a foreigner.

The heart of our troubles is our personal conflict. As personifications of the non-verbal Unified Field we, today, uniquely invent and learn to communicate accurately through evidence-based stories. In and around us, the Field does not understand them because it is not story literate. In addition, it can't respond or deal with any mystical or inaccurate stories that separate us from it. This makes Nature in and around us vulnerable to any story's disconnectedness in whatever we relate to. It makes our body into two bodies 1) our "story communication body" and 2) our "non-verbal, non-story body" that is the life of Planet Earth manifesting itself as us.

Earth experiences its life in and around us as an organic love-in while our stories teach us that to survive we should sense it as a football game or war that we must constantly win against it. This produces additional stories like "Life sucks and then you die," or "The world is more divided and dangerous, we need a unifying force, a unifying source like a political Michael Jackson or an attack by aliens.

That source of unity is now available as GreenWave-54. We have human rights to it. and our education violates them and us by withholding it .

Our nature-disconnected stories trespass Earth and it cannot complain with words so we do not understand it or what it shares with us. GreenWave-54, also called the GreenWave Equation, is a Rosetta Stone for this catastrophe and its misery factors that violate the right to life of our Planet and us. It is a sensory tool that empowers any individual to speak with and for the Earth by creating moments in natural areas that let Earth teach us what we need to know. Earth accomplishes this through our 54 sensory attraction/loves that its Unified Field "invented" and are us. Earth uses them to communicate with and balance its relationships with its life as us. (<u>The Hidden Organic Remedy, 2013</u>).

We are all in the same living planet boat, Earth, because we are it and when you tip one end you rock the other. Although objective science helps us deal with the harmful effects of our tipping, it is also the runaway culprit that is doing the tipping. It needs GreenWave-54 because GreenWave is a social technology that enables higher education to make our limited objectivity bind and blend with subjective phenomena through 54 unified field natural attractions that are whole-life facts of life.

By using, mainly, the "objective" 15 percent of our 54-sense whole-life intelligence we have a whole-life IQ of 15, that of an idiot. When we are educated to think, feel and relate with our additional 46 sense "subjective" senses we enjoy a whole-life IQ of 100 and our troubles subside.

GreenWave-54 helps us guide objective science into producing balanced, whole life relationships. Omitting it is like taking a broken computer to a blacksmith for repairs while in denial that a blacksmith's expertise is inappropriate for computer maintenance. His repair job months earlier injured it; that's why it doesn't work now.

Objective Science won't accept that homeostasis works throughout Nature because in every time/space moment, the life dance of the Universe in all things consciously loves to be part of the central Unified Field, as well as simultaneously loves to enter whatever new, diverse, relationship is attractive in that moment that will strengthen the Field. These two attraction directions continually dance between and balance each other to produce the equilibrium of homeostasis. It is the heartbeat of Earth's life in all things. Any researcher who makes 54 sense connection with natural areas for a period of time can recognize this.

Because contact with <u>natural areas for sixty years</u> has taught me how to consistently register GreenWave-54 and learn from it, it guides my life and evidently sustains my wellness and happiness more powerfully than what is average. Scientifically, it is the source. At age 87 my health, physical abilities and medical tests tend to affirm this or maybe I'm just very lucky (Cohen, 1993). I think it's because Greenwave Unified Field contact is central to how I fulfill my 54 senses, and I can be a frustrating enigma to folks who don't do this. And, yes, using GreenWave 54 natural area grok connections I connect with long dead leaders who I invite to join me in natural areas. There and then I update them about today's science and technologies. In return I obtain their coping wisdom from these wild areas. This is no surprise, this is where they grokked it, too.

I am delighted that my GreenWave-54 art and science empowers anyone to join the pure love and aliveness of *natural attraction*. Without using stories or labels, it is conscious of itself loving to become more attractive by building additional natural attraction relationships that are reasonable.

> Labels or stories that disconnect us from this fundamental unifying process produce our discontents and their pain. This is because moment by moment we each help to survive the same attractive/beautiful Earth that we sense and feel in any moment.

> It is horrific nonsense to deprive young folks of the GreenWave-54 remedy while knowing that their lives will suffer its absence.

We are educated to be prejudiced, to attach or addict ourselves to 8 of our 54 senses that together we call our "objective" thinking. However, this process omits the "subjective". It is the 46 other sensitivity intelligences that we share with Nature and that hold the natural world in its self-correcting balance and beauty, in and around us, as us.

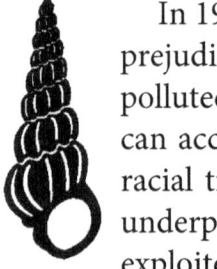 In 1983 I wrote, "Many Americans trigger hurtful social conflicts by relating prejudicially to women, minorities and children. Now we discover that our polluted relationship with the life of Nature is also founded in prejudice, and can accordingly be improved. For every minority group complaint, for every racial transgression, for inhumane acts against people, plants or animals, for underpaid workers and unhealthy work or home environments, for each exploited student, civil rights offense or warlike deed, for sexist acts or emotional or economic blows, the is a matching or more serious transgression that has taken place against the life of our planet due to our denial of our prejudice against its nature. We don't rectify these social problems because they are not just human problems, they are short-circuit life problems. They are love and life challenges that are resolved in society only as we scientifically correct our prejudicial story about the life of Nature. That story injures us because Nature's life is our life. We are disturbed because our nature-disconnected stories are disturbing us.

Many times I've worked with folks who love Nature and say they are "turned off" by science and technology yet they use computers, roads, cars, eyeglasses, hotels etc. to attend the workshop. They come away with a different impression after they experience GreenWave-54 as a supportive, whole-life science that responsibly strengthens our spirit and happiness via accurate story connections with Nature that help us reduce our excessive dependencies on artifacts. It makes sense that *helping the self-correcting way that nature works flow through us corrects our nature-disconnected thinking and relationships.*

We cannot win the battle to increase the well-being of the planet's life and ours, without strengthening our inborn ability to love all of life. As GreenWave-54 enables our body, mind, and spirit to recognize each of us to be a unique personification of the Unified Field, we recover our missing 54 natural attraction/love sensory bonds with Nature, in and around us. They are our greatest hope in reversing Earth Overshoot because we do not give the life of earth the rights to legally protect itself. We must fight to protect it and we seldom fight to save what we do not love enough. We win that fight by ferociously regenerating integrity through the substitution of GreenWave-54 consensual relationships for the destructive aspects of the factory whistle, the school bell and non-organic authorities.

Although the GreenWave-54 process has been available since 1972, it remains today foreign to or obnoxious in Education and Counseling procedures. Easily adding it to every aspect of these and any other disciplines would significantly reduce most problems in less than six years. The Internet makes this rapid time frame possible and the process would easily pay for itself through an 85 percent reduction in expenditures for our present "15 percent effective" efforts to enjoy the wellness of peace and sanity.

What we desperately need is this class action suit to prevail. It would legislate that Education get itself out of denial and manifest our human rights to whole-life relationships. As John Dewey noted, "We only think when confronted by a problem." The decision of this jury regarding GreenWave-54 is the "problem" you can produce *to the benefit of all*. Education and Counseling in any discipline would have to be GreenWave-54 accredited and 'Certified Organic' as is my online degree program now.

WITNESS 22 SUMMARY: by 85% GW-54 unchains our inborn ability to love all of life.

The senses, being the explorers of the world, open the way to knowledge.
                                        - Maria Montessori

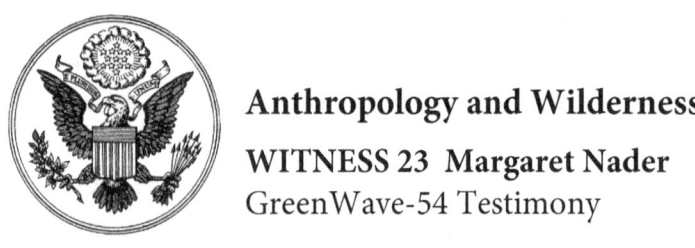

Anthropology and Wilderness

WITNESS 23 Margaret Nader
GreenWave-54 Testimony

The historical cause of Overshoot and its violation of our rights is that the unified field loved humanity into a being designed to live in the tropics of organism Earth. There, extreme seasons did not exist, fur was not needed and food and medicine was available in the wild year round. This geographical fact is the origin of the Garden of Eden story where Nature in the story-less raw of its beauty and balance supported humanity.

As nomads wandered into non-tropical habitats, most discovered how to let Nature there support them in balance. Other groups invented and conveyed technological knowledge and stories that let them convert any non-tropical environment into tools or a built environment that artificially provided tropic-like conditions. Survival became inventing, attaching to and rewarding unbalanced survival stories and technologies along with the individuals who could best conquer and convert so-called hostile natural environments into fabricated indoor tropics. Our 54 natural attraction/love senses were hurtfully disconnected from the unified field in natural areas and bonded to stories and people who, by rewards and punishments, conquered nature, in and around us. This was accompanied by "lemon" stories that attached Nature's love for humanity to imaginary beings who existed in imaginary places elsewhere. They were, and remain, fantasies that support our nature-disconnected, thinking and relationships while soothing our stress and abandonment anxieties that result from our excessive Planet Mother disconnection. These nature-disconnected stories caused our body, mind, and spirit to become more and more destructively addicted to profiting by creating artificiality. Our natures have been disconnected from 54 senses; institutions, science, and technologies have advanced while eliminating the balancing controls that are found in all natural areas (Cohen 2011).

Nature in us has responded to its continued disconnection and abuse with discomforting symptoms that signal we must reconnect. These are our discontents that we tranquilize, stress about or act out. It's like the 9/11 Twin Tower catastrophe is a reprisal for centuries of our hi-tech, conquer Nature story assaulting Nature in individuals and cultures. We can't injure our Earth life form that we are part of without us being injured.

GreenWave-54 reverses our runaway trespass of Nature, in and around us, by hands-on reconnecting our personhood to its origins and fulfillments in the unified field, backyard, or backcountry and in each other. We develop a stalwart integrity that stops us from violating any individual's legal rights to life in balance. As an Anthropologist, I think GreenWave-54 is essential because we still do not give legal rights to Nature itself, biologically or spiritually. Instead, construction after construction, the natural world becomes meat for our grinder instead of a protected outdoor cathedral that can bring our psyche and relationships into the equilibrium of wellness. Industrial society has become a cancer. Higher education illegally deprives us of our right to an education that addresses and prevents this cancer's cause and remedy.

It is like Industrial Society has emotionally attached us to drive an advanced technology automobile. As we speed this 2-ton steel missile down the highway we see in that it leads directly into a group of people having a picnic in a beautiful park yet all we can do is hope or pray that the car will stop as, in fear and dismay, we scream "whoa," as if it is a horse. This behavior is unscientific and obsolete. It does not stop the car and it wreaks havoc. This disaster occurs because Industrial Society fails to teach us that it has also invented brakes for the car and how to use them. For example, today, most scientists agree that Industrial Society is producing climate change yet these same scientists don't know how or why we continue to do this or how to stop. Sadly, this shortcoming is typical of most of our leaders and relationships. It is what makes us produce our runaway personal, social and environmental problems. We don't learn that GreenWave-54 is an organic technology of behavior *brake,* how to use it and how to integrate it into our relationships.

WITNESS 23 SUMMARY: by 85% GW-54 reverses our trespasses of Nature in and around us.

> *The world is not to be put in order, the world is order. It is for us to put ourselves in unison with this order.*
>
> **- Henry Miller**

Personal Field Journal Report: **Fulfilling What Life Asks of Me.**

WITNESS 24 Sally Goodwin

GreenWave-54 Testimony:

I was attracted at first to the field of flowers and noticed that while most of them had many flowers on one stem, one plant had only one yellow flower on it and I changed my direction because it attracted me. It brought to mind a situation in the past when I made a decision to take a new path, to change and let go of a situation where I was overly responsible and causing myself and others pain. I am now finding myself at a similar crossroad and yet my awareness has come very quickly and transition is very rapid. In the past I taught nursing on the Navajo reservation. I was cut off from sources of nourishment and support being 300 miles from main campus and a worldview away.

I experience my ancestral trauma through the trauma of my students as they/we attempted without support to span the gap of what I would now describe as nature-connected vs. nature-separated thinking. I am now experiencing a cut-off of support in my present nursing practice where I suddenly do not feel safe, supported or centered. Untrained staff, reimbursement issues, and chaos prevail. I keep habitually thinking if I were more…, patient, kind, understanding, smarter, faster, and so forth. Then I recognize this feeling- aha!! Here it is again- well -"thank you" to this field of plants and again to this process. You have freed me from being habitually enslaved to put energy toward my area of injury. Rather, I will put energy toward that which nourishes and supports me. I will, as the plant one blossom, expose the beauty of my one yellow flower-the pure and fragile essence of my true nature- only revealing this beauty to that which supports me and save further energy for continued growth and preparation as I follow alternate paths. I am grateful to the plants for the reminder of my freedom to focus inward, to seek intelligently  through GreenWave-54 natural love attractions that nourish and support me in fulfilling what life asks of me. This could be my behaviorial epigenetics working.

WITNESS 24 SUMMARY: by 85% GW-54 heightens self-nourishing and supportive energies.

The greatest science in the world, in heaven and on earth, is love.
- **Mother Teresa**

Addictive Prejudice Against Nature

WITNESS 25 Toby Salvidore

In 1984 Dr. Cohen wrote that it was reasonable for our prejudice against nature to be identified for the prejudice, evisceration or rape, that it was (Cohen, 1983). Sadly, he remembered a young child he knew at Camp Turkey Point in 1945, Michael Schwerner, who, as an adult, was one of the three civil rights workers murdered by the Ku Klux Klan in 1964. He felt that Michael did not risk putting his life on the line just to correct a misunderstanding or to complete incomplete information. Michael's rational passion called to him because racial prejudice was hurting the rights of human life, people of color were being hanged from trees. Cohen recognized that, similarly, our prejudice against nature had wounded or killed the web of life in the ongoing and excessive nature-insensitive war that industrial society had, for profit, secretly declared against defenseless and story-deficient nature. Unless people felt the horror, unfairness, and pain inflicted by this war, they would remain desensitized and prejudiced. As the protectors of civil rights, peace, labor, equality, and social justice demonstrated, the correct word, prejudice, brought the passion of the heart into some people's reasoning. Like "lemon memories" it motivated them to act, especially to support and defend the lives of themselves and people and things they loved.

In his 2015 Encyclical on Nature and elsewhere, Pope Francis has said that the violence that exists in the human heart is also manifest in the symptoms of illness that we see in the Earth, the water, the air and in living things. If we destroy Creation, Creation will destroy us. The environment is intimately connected to our care for each other. We are faced with one complex crisis, which is both social and environmental. The rich and powerful shut themselves up within self-enclosed enclaves, compulsively consuming the latest goods to feed the emptiness within their hearts, while ignoring the plight of the poor. The poor are on the run from natural disasters and degraded habitats, shunted to the bottom of the world's pile of problems with decreasing access to its natural resources. The destruction of the Rainforest is a sin. Humanity has become enamored of another apple in the Garden of Eden, a forbidden fruit to innovative technology, but the sin remains the same: hubris. The earth, our home, is beginning to look more and more like an immense pile of filth.

Like the Pope, more and more authorities recognize the full story of equality, that humanity is part of nature and to harm one harms the other. The family of "man" is in denial that it is killing its biological mother under the flag of economic growth. We suffer our aberrant behavior because we have no funeral to safely express our grief from the loss of our whole-of-life family members.   For centuries, authorities have held similar stories about the equality of individuals no matter their race, sex, religion or economic status. Advances have been made in honoring this equality, but sadly, these come at Nature's cost because the advances don't include the natural world as a family member so we further exploit it as an emotionally satisfying pacifier. This results from our Society's ultimate authority being the disconnection and prejudice in our Nature-disconnected stories rather than their support of GreenWave-54 contact with Nature's Unified Field.

Prejudice can be seen as an unreasonable pre-judging attitude that is, due to bonding, unusually resistant to rational influence and bonding is often addictive. GreenWave-54 gives any individual the ability to discover and deal with the violence that results from authorities not recognizing that they are emotionally bonded to hold a cultural prejudice against nature that has painfully disconnected their and our mentality from the benefits of the Unified Field.

With respect to our higher education leaders and their prejudice against nature, we are, today, in real life, in far worse shape than were the subjects of the astonishing Milgram studies of 1961 (Milgram, 1974). In those studies, a supervisor committed the subjects to administer increasingly painful electrical shocks to people who answered meaningless questions incorrectly. The subjects could hear the shock-recipients in another room but they could not see them. They were fully aware that they cried out in increasing pain, anguish and protest as the experiment progressed and the shock voltage increased. Despite this, they sometimes applied the shocks even after they recognized that the recipient had died. **What the subjects did not know was the alleged recipients did not actually receive the shocks, that their cries were recordings.**

What was not predicted was that although some subjects cringed and complained, most would not stop hurting the shock recipients as the voltage they applied and responding cries increased and the supervisor urged them to continue. The subjects, instead, responded to the authority of the supervisor. It was as if the subjects were insane. They could not act reasonably from their senses when they had the choice to disobey a voluntarily accepted authority. These senses had been numbed if not deadened. This experiment was recently repeated and the results were the same.

We are in greater trouble now than were the Milgram subjects and participants forty years ago. This is because today the authority phenomenon is not a study. It is real life and true to the lives of most contemporary people, especially young people; they are the most vulnerable. The life that our authorities have us shocking and hurting is the life of our Planet and Nature, in and around us. This is authentic. We know it full well and we see and feel the disastrous personal, social and environmental effects of the traumatic stress it inflicts. However, we don't stop obeying our outer and inner authorities so our detrimental impact increases each year.

We are painfully aware that we are subject to stories from profit driven, nature-exploiting authorities, directives and advertisements that unbalance us. They include the misguided information that induces, pays, applauds or addicts us to excessively use products that secretly administer lethal shocks to the life of our Planet and Nature, in and about us, now and in the future. It begs three important questions for each individual, "Who is the Boss of you?" "What disasters are you placing on your children?" "How will we ever find GreenWave-54 if we continue to hide it?"

As part of Nature we suffer the pain we are goaded into inflicting on Nature while, be we administrator, scientist or client in denial, our prejudice against Nature deceives us to say that we can't find a major way to stop doing this, even though GreenWave-54 is available.

Our helplessness and its outrageous Earth Overshoot effects occur because our Society pays and promotes authorities to fire or admonish us for not doing their nature-disconnected biddings. In addition, these "bosses" encourage us not to believe what our 54 natural senses convey to us. Instead, the bosses say we must listen to their erroneous messages as well as spend, on average, over 95 percent of our time and felt-sense thinking and relating out of tune with how Nature's Unified Field works.

Due to our excessive disconnection from Nature we seldom hear, feel, or make sense of the pain and disorders we inflict on the natural world, in and about us. Instead, unhappily, we endure them or try to pass "Band-Aid" laws that forbid their continuance rather than GreenWave-54 address and remove their source.

We become so attuned to being attached to, or cultural-object subjects of our authorities that part of our mentality subconsciously takes on their role. They become our inner authority stories. We not only can't stop listening to real administrators, when they are absent we listen to their images and instruction stories that we don't realize we have unconsciously fixed in our mind. Meanwhile our 54 senses scream, "Stop your shocking behavior. We are aware of what is happening to us and the whole of nature." Our senses are sensible enough to know that we can't share the life of Earth and not be sick when it is sick.

We can't realistically enjoy full trust and satisfactions from relationships when we know they are not honorable because we can see that they are not in balance. Even the best of researchers are not immune to this phenomenon. They can discover a truth and at the same time act as if it was not true. For example, although the faculties of most universities have the opportunity to add GreenWave-54 to each of their disciplines, they choose not to while they address themselves as "honorable". Who is the boss of them? If you don't believe our crazy attachments to destructive authorities is addictive, just try and stop it. As Chellis Glendinning said, *My name is Chellis and I am in recovery from Western Civilization.*

I have seen where the connection of our 54 senses to their natural attraction origins in the Unified Field reasonably revives, restores and energizes them organically as well as frees them from their destructive attachments in Industrial Society. In Nature's Unified Field, mutually produced and attractive "Thank you for your love and care," good feeling fulfillments are always available. This connection in people and natural areas reduces our prejudice against Nature. We become more sensible, healthy and open to reasonable change. Our rights to our freedom from excessiveness, drug use, conflict, crime, stress and illness strengthen as a result.

 **The Department of Justice can't enforce justice** for Nature because the prejudice against Nature authority of the U.S. Constitution gives Nature no legal rights. Similarly, we are affected by the past and present prejudiced against Nature "Bosses" in our lives along with their violation of our rights and reasoning as demonstrated in the Milgram studies.

Our dilemma is that our addiction counselors are unknowingly addicted to our nature-disconnecting stories. For example: August 6, 2007: Researchers gave a group of 3-5-year-old children two identical servings of many different kinds of food. The only difference between the two servings was that one was wrapped in a McDonald's wrapper, the other in a plain wrapper. Overwhelmingly, the children said the identical food placed in the McDonald's wrapper tasted better (Robinson 2007). At this early age their psyche, including their sense of taste had been socialized, misled and corrupted through branding. This would remain in their adulthood and produce resistance to more reasonable products. ***This is the present state of GreenWave-54 as well. It helps explain why our troubles are increasing.***

Bonding to GreenWave-54 is not an addiction because its positive rather than negative effects produce whole life happiness, enlightenment and relationships rather than soldiers of our wayward society.

GreenWave-54 is available as a counselor to help us make the Unified Field a wise, supportive and trustable Boss instead of continuing to omit its contributions. When added to meditation it reaches senses that have been "McDonaled", warped senses that meditating may not reach.   How can any of us glue differing things together in beneficial unification if we don't learn how to open up the glue bottle and apply the glue in it that can accomplish this?

It is obvious that each of us has a right to life that is being violated by our prejudiced against Nature stories. Through GreenWave-54 their removal gives Earth's self-correcting abilities the time and space to recover and restore Earth and us.

This jury can promote the opportunity for the self-evident right to life-in-balance by us as well as by all other forms of life. Simply decide to let this issue go to trial. Be reasonable. Give the law a chance to reverse our prejudice against Nature by at least requiring higher education to make GreenWave-54 skills a requirement for college admission, as are math and language skills now.

WITNESS 25 SUMMARY: by 85% GW-54 reduces our addictive prejudice against Nature.

The Earth is our mother. Whatever befalls the earth, befalls the sons of the earth. If men spit upon the ground, they spit upon themselves.

Humankind has not woven the web of life. We are but one thread within it. All things are bound together. All things connect.

The Earth does not belong to man; man belongs to Earth. What is man without the beasts? If all the beasts were gone, men would die from great loneliness of spirit, for whatever happens to the beasts also happens to the man.
                                    - Chief Seattle/Ted Perry/The Preacher King
                                    (Ecclesiastes 3:19 Revised Standard Versi

Sensing Herbal Remedies

WITNESS 26 Lorie Flower
GreenWave-54 Testimony

My experience as an herbalist has lead me down Nature's path. I am always looking for ways to enhance well-being and I have worked with groups of people, some in the professional sports world, as I explored adding GreenWave-54 to compliment my herbal remedies. A scientific study with weight loss provided a measured improvement in my clients' personal well-being as I found it did for others in depression, post-traumatic stress syndrome and physical injury. Attractions they discovered in GreenWave-54 gave individuals a wholeness with nature that led to better recuperation. Each person became more in touch with sensory connections that are vital to a whole body-whole earth consciousness and that process is a significant contribution to services provided by the herbal remedies profession. No other wide-ranged item appeared to be as effective for the array of measured recuperative changes. All beings have the ability to benefit from the GreenWave experience and people should be educated to enjoy this natural right.

WITNESS 26 SUMMARY: by 85% GW-54 empowers recuperation from post-traumatic stress.

No medicine can cure the damage caused by disregarding the inner intelligence with which we are gifted.

- Renu Chaudhary

Personal Field Journal Report: **Being the Unified Field**

WITNESS 27 Steve Rector
GreenWave-54 Testimony:

While near Guss Island, a protected natural area, I began my first experience with GreenWave-54. David, our mentor, introduced four of us to it by having us validate that whatever our senses experienced in any moment was an undeniable, self-evident fact for us that we did not need to defend. This included that we could sense that we had many more than five senses operating as we spoke and we identified some of them: hearing, distance, gravity, self, literacy, consciousness, aliveness, humor and reason. Our sense of reason noted that the story that we have 5 senses was inaccurate and limiting. It also validated that nowhere here or in our education could we find any evidence of Nature communicating through stories or labels.

To help us know Nature as it knew its nameless and speechless self, we recognized that our attraction to visit this natural area without harming it signaled that we had the area's consent to spent five minutes quietly in the woods there identifying each thing that we became aware of as "nameless" or "story-less". We then got together and shared what we sensed and felt from doing this. We discovered that by dropping our labels and stories what one person said they had experienced each of us sensed as well in this moment for moment-by-moment we were still unified in and by the forest. This seemed reasonable because we were and are all part of Nature.

We helped each other realize that our love or attraction to Nature was our 54 senses registering the Unified Higgs Boson Field bringing all things into attracted, connected belonging in the Universe's time and space of each new moment (A new Copernicun revolution, 2012). Then, we spent five minutes by ourselves labeling things we became aware of, including ourselves, as "Unified Field Attraction Love".

When we got together again as a group, a stronger unifying ecstasy was present. Now our senses of love, trust, place, community and time were apparent while being intensified by the forest community. Folks shared how this same feeling of well-being had helped them and others when they were ill and that some folks had addicted to artificially producing that feeling by using drugs or alcohol. These wonderfully detached them from their stories while bringing them relief or emotional rewards but they were accompanied by detrimental aftereffects. GreenWave-54 was suggested as a healthy substitute for these satisfactions. The things people now sensed were

- how amazingly diverse Nature was,
- how we loved being aware of and in Nature,
- how each thing in a natural area was a unique and attractive individual, including each of us,
- how it felt good that everything was right there to experience and love in the moment,
- that we felt relieved by not having to label things "correctly" or at all,
- that we discovered many new things about Nature by removing stories and labels from them and then we felt closer to them.
- that a "brightening" or vibrancy of things took place after a while when we called them "Nameless." We could hear things we didn't hear moments earlier.
- feeling a greater belongingness to everything when we called ourselves "nameless".
- even our advanced meditation processes benefited from a new, unifying, natural dimension.
- calling human-built structures and effects "runaway blueprints" gave us more motivation to reasonably control of them.

We walked back to the beginning of the trail labeling things we experienced as "love," "attraction" or "unified field" and we felt much closer to each other than when we started. Then David had us pinch ourselves until it hurt so we stopped. We explored how the sense of pain was not a negative rather it was an attraction. It was Nature's attraction to signal us to find more satisfying and reasonable attractions and we recognized that sensations of anxiety, depression and anguish did this as well.

We validated that moment-by-moment everything was attractively connected and as one as part of the Unified Field of the Universe throughout our walk. When we sensed that plants or we were alive, the Earth and Universe also had to be alive for everything was the identical essence of aliveness in that moment. David mentioned that humanity had invented time so everything wouldn't happen all at once because, since it did not need time to make stories, in nature everything was instantaneous.

We ended up looking at clouds as they moved across the sky into beautiful new shapes and we felt harmony and peace knowing we were doing the same with them and each other, no matter our cultural or genetic differences. We noted that people in the middle of a city could do this with clouds, parks or weeds as well. Then David distributed sheets with the 54 senses listed on them and activities we could do to strengthen them (Cohen, M. J., 2016).

What fascinated me was that using GreenWave-54 we learned all this through trustable experiences in Nature, the real thing, in less than an hour because what we were learning we could sense and feel right there around and in us, not from just a book or lecture about it. We were being reality, not just abstracting it with stories, right or wrong. We were helping our senses remember what they already knew and were as we gave them safe time and space to connect with it. At my school it would have taken a four-month science and philosophy course to get the same results if that was even possible. Can an indoor course ever substitute for learning how Nature works from direct sensory connection with authentic Nature, the fountainhead of authority in how it works? Don't we need its presence as we move from one moment into the next?

WITNESS 27 SUMMARY: by 85% GW-54 enables sensing ourselves as the Unified Field.

> *The only source of knowledge is experience*
> **-Albert Einstein**

> *Mister President, the unity we need is our 54 senses finding it in a natural area.*
> **- Michael J. Cohen**

> *One touch of Nature makes the whole world kin.*
> **- William Shakespeare**

Political Implications

WITNESS 28 Roger Elliot
GreenWave-54 Testimony:

I offer this jury that legal precedence has been set to use GreenWave 54 in to protect people's right to live reasonable and happy lives (Grange #966, 2015):

JUNE 3, 2015
A RESOLUTION CONCERNING THE OVERSHOOT OF EARTH'S CARRYING CAPACITY

WHEREAS, the Declaration of Purposes of the National Grange, adopted by the St. Louis session of the National Grange, February 11, 1874 stated, "We shall endeavor…to buy less and produce more, in order to make our farms self-sustaining; to diversify our crops and crop no more than we can cultivate; to condense the weight of our exports, selling less in the bushel and more on hoof and in fleece, less in lint and more in warp and woof;…; to discountenance the credit system, the mortgage system, the fashion system, and every other system tending to prodigality and bankruptcy" (National Grange, 1874); and

WHEREAS, many of the natural resources of Earth are finite, and are not being created at the rate they are being consumed; and

WHEREAS, many past civilizations have gone bankrupt and are no more, after overshooting the carrying capacities of their regions; and

WHEREAS, our current world-wide civilization is not immune to natural laws concerning the carrying capacity of Earth; and

WHEREAS, many of our current agricultural, industrial and financial activities tend toward "prodigality and bankruptcy" in regard to sustaining our civilization and our planet's life and integrity; and

WHEREAS, Scientists recognize Planet Earth is a living organism and that all members of its plant, animal, mineral and energy kingdoms are alive in balance;

THEREFORE BE IT RESOLVED, that we must act as ambassadors of Earth to guide humanity away from its excesses which lead to an overshoot of Earth's ability to meet our material and emotional needs; and

BE IT FURTHER RESOLVED, that the San Juan Island Grange #966 offer the tools to accomplish this worthy goal to its members and to the public (The National Grange, 1874)

Passed Unanimously, June 3, 2015

SOURCE INFORMATION:
Earth, as a living organism, as understood through the application of GreenWave-54: Albert Einstein's Unified Field NNIAAL Equation
http://www.ecopsych.com/saneearth.html
www.mjcnow.info
www.ecopsych.com/zombie2.html
http://www.ecopsych.com/journalwarranty.html
The Declaration of Purposes of the National Grange, adopted by the St. Louis session of the National Grange, February 11, 1874:
http://www.oocities.org/cannongrange/declaration_purposes.html

WITNESS 28 SUMMARY: by 85% GW-54 institutionally increases people/planet sanity

How few there are who have courage enough to own their faults, or resolution enough to mend them

- Benjamin Franklin

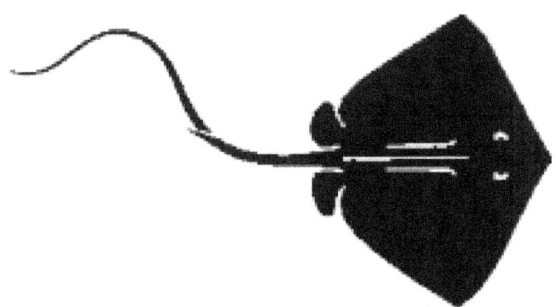

The Prosecutor's Charge to the Jury

 **Robert Goldwater, Prosecutor**

Before I read to you the key parts of GreenWave-54 from its online edition (Einstein, A., 2014-2016), I'm going to describe for you what is at stake in this hearing and how you can help our present "justice for the few with power" become personal, social, and environmental justice for all of life.

Although in 1776 the Declaration of Independence declared we have an inalienable right to life and the pursuit of happiness, the 1787 Constitution did not declare or give us our right to life. We have it from the Fourteenth Amendment in 1868, eighty years later. Neither happiness nor Nature appears in the Constitution.

I again remind you that undeniably we scientifically live in the time and space of the life of our planet. When withheld speech by some parts of society damage the health of its life, they damage the health of our health, too, and they can be held legally responsible for their acts by those whose rights, including property, have been violated.

As GreenWave-54 scientifically demonstrates, the natural life of our Planet and Universe is the self-correcting and pure foundation of our lives. We have excessively separated ourselves from it. Without its wisdom, process and support as our foundation we have created a void in our psyche and corrupted ourselves as well as Nature at every level of relating. GreenWave-54 can help us fill this void with natural attraction love and correct this corruption in our foundations as well as in incidents found throughout society. The defendants have prevented us from doing this by withholding GreenWave-54 information.

Note that many people excessively profit from our corruption. They oppose GreenWave-54 because it is free and it gives us the tools and ability to correct the warp in the way we habitually felt-sense think and relate, including the anti-nature warp that is the root of our troubles. Attending to the disorders that the warp produces is a major industry. However, as the witnesses claim, profiteers would not be against it if they were engaged in it and profiting from it in a good way. Even this hearing is possibly corrupt. You do not know if or how many of the 23 of you have or will be approached by special interests to not let this complaint go to trial. It would be no surprise if you do not trust the Justice Department or even me in this regard, no less the trial by jury that you can sanction. In reality it is all for sale. Is it even possible for your sense of reason to make good sense of this grand jury hearing about how we have warped our 54 senses if your 54 senses are warped?

What you can do is make the trial happen rather than not happen. Significant potential for good is found whenever justice occurs especially justice for all including the web of life.

The Defendants are accused of illegally depriving us of the benefits of GreenWave-54. To increase and strengthen fairness, the United States Department of Justice wants the law to force the Defendants to make the GreenWave-54 benefit available as well as pay for damages incurred from the Defendant's negligent omission of it that deprives us of many constitutional and human rights.

As the witnesses have just testified, by being educated to put on and wear GreenWave-54 glasses we can relate to the world more realistically and harmoniously from the heart, in the same way that the math-science of Copernicus helped us to benefit from knowing the Sun, not the Earth, as the center of our solar system. GreenWave-54 enables us to felt-sense think and relate to ourselves, each other and the world for what simultaneously we actually are as the whole of life. Scientifically, we are, moment-by-moment, a singular, alive Earth and the aliveness of its Universe that we also call Nature, that can speak. Without a story, it produces its own space and time and is held together everywhere each moment by natural attractions that include an attraction to expand or grow more attractive. This is an attraction that our 54 senses register and support and actually are. If we don't want to eviscerate our life and our rights to it, we must learn to speak GreenWave-54.

As human beings we are each a unique personification of Organism Earth as it flows around and through us and becomes us. We are each cells of it that hold in common our attractive genetic ability to build relationships through abstract stories. However, we are vulnerable to unreasonable "lemon story" inaccuracies and prejudices about our world. Attachments to these stories mislead us to excessively separate from our planet, to habitually act destructively, and to suffer accordingly as does  Earth as well. Our scientifically inaccurate stories that disintegrate the whole of life deprive us of our human rights as happy citizens of Earth and the intelligence of its universal aliveness. As the witnesses have described:

Our senses are the undeniable self-evidence that we register, believe and relate to the world. When they are lost or distorted what can be trusted?

Our 54 natural senses normally attract our life to Earth's unconditional love of all things.

 We suffer our challenging problems because our stories teach us to detach our senses from Nature's self-correcting ways and attach them instead to our artificial, conquering, Nature-disconnected stories and technologies.

Our detachments emotionally tear our body, mind and spirit from Earth's unifying 54 sense embrace, and it from ours.

The pain and abandonment caused by our severance from Nature and its love for us deteriorates our collective and personal outlooks.

Our destructive separation from Nature makes us want. We feel that there is never enough of anything, especially love.

We addictively fill our love gap with material possessions and artificial relationships and can't stop even though we are aware that in the process our excessiveness is dismantling planet/person life and our whole life support from it.

GreenWave-54 reverses our disorders by creating moments that let Nature's conscious attraction love help us produce mutually supportive whole life satisfactions, enlightenment and relationships with Nature around and in us.

Our human rights include the rights and freedom of Nature, within us and as us, to be recognized as a person (PNC, 2007), to equality, to security, to public hearing, and to remedies by competent tribunal.

Our tribunal today can strengthen people's rights to love and be loved; to freedom of opinion, belief and information; to get an education; to be considered innocent; to life and freedom from degrading treatment.

Our inquest today can reduce the huge economic costs as well as the physical and mental pain we suffer from our attachments to nature-disconnected stories. They produce our racial, religious and gender prejudices, destructive stress, unfairness and inequality, mental illness, corruption, abusiveness, violence, addiction, rape, excessiveness, environmental degradation and poverty. Each infringes upon our right to pursue happiness by deteriorating our ability and freedom to do so.

By requiring GreenWave-54 everywhere this jury will give Nature in all of us personal rights to life and happiness that we can use to help protect Nature in the environment that our stories have given no rights. This will increase Justice for all members of the web of life, not just us, as well as reverse and heal the miseries we presently suffer from 150-400 percent Earth Overshoot.

Long-term happiness is the feeling that biologically comes into play whenever any of our 54 natural attraction senses are fulfilled in a reasonable way. It is the joy of life whose right to pursue it is specifically stated in the Declaration of Independence but then omitted in the Constitution. The Plaintiffs simply want the government to live up to the Declaration of Independence and the Constitution by legally giving them the knowledge of and access to GreenWave-54 as part of government regulated education from pre-school on, no less, higher education. This is the highest purpose of higher education and although higher education institutions acknowledge this, they are prejudiced to deprive us of the scientifically accurate GreenWave-54 tools we need to make it happen.

Tapping into the unified energy field of the Universe through GreenWave-54 enables us to understand and act from who and where we are by removing the walls of alienation, environmental destruction, ignorance and despair that result from our intellect's estrangement from our universal aliveness and its sensory wisdom. Because GreenWave-54 has ancient sensory roots in our planet and human experience as well as the frontiers of modern science, it helps us transform our discontents into the immense unifying powers of reasonable, 54-sense love for life in balance and beauty. It lets our civilized love and its discontents be improved by connecting with natural love.

For the reasons I have stated in this inquest I charge the 23 of you to find that the defendants must face the investigations, fairness and decisions of a trial by judge and jury. Your biggest challenge here is the same as mine. We all have to overcome our nature-disconnected training by the defendants, our possible attachments to non-scientific stories that warp your reasoning as a jury member. In a natural area the GreenWave Unified Attraction Field (GUAF) is registered and known in 54 sensory ways. However, mainly three of the 54 are used in my presentation of the case to you in this courtroom: consciousness, reason and language. This case deals with an immense runaway threat to the well-being of life on Earth as it's attraction conscious wisdom has loved it into its balanced and beautiful being, moment-by-moment for almost 14 billion years. In the nature-separated confines of this courtroom, this presentation is like a powerful military tank that our reasoning is trying to control by inappropriately using three-sense sling shot and bow and arrow stories to stop the tank. We are limited to this because our "military tank" nature-disconnected education and counseling by the defendants have restricted how we think, feel and relate. Years ago they probably crippled the scientifically reasonable thinking of most jury members and left you with ancient ways of knowing that are inappropriate for contemporary decision making. This is why mystical or religious testimony is invalid in science or courtrooms.

For you to be as sensible and fair as possible here, I'd like you to use the checklist (below) to help you bring more of your 54 natural senses into your awareness and take what you feel is true from them into consideration with respect to you considering the testimony of the witnesses. This gives 54-sense, whole life science a way to level the playing field and make a reasonable decision possible. Remember that in a natural area each of these 54 senses and feelings is a fact of whole life that, to be fair, you should not omit in your considerations here. This checklist may help you make a more scientifically valid 54 sense decision.

CHECKLIST

GreenWave Unified Field Aliveness (GUFA) manifests itself as 54 natural attraction senses in you. Does their GUFA register from the witnesses that

( ) You are in and part of our scientifically determined universe right now.

( ) Our scientific Universe works because it is designed by us using the same logic and rules of evidence that produce the excellence of today's objective, technological world and its benefits that our contemporary lives depend on.

( ) Scientifically, since the beginning of its natural attraction's consciousness to exist as material life, 13.8 billion years ago, the alive essence of the life of the Universe, (the Higgs Boson Unified Field), *has been attracted to sustain itself* and survive by creating its own time and space dance moment after moment. *All things are held together by attraction/love.* They dance to produce *now attraction that includes us as dancers.*

( ) The aliveness of the Universe and all things in it, including you, only exists in this moment, not in the past or the future. The latter are only stories or memories. *In this GUFA moment* they contain and attach us to the past and/or the future.

( ) GUFA/us loves to continue to exist (survive) by self-building its next balanced whole-life moment of time and space as it flows into it, lives in it and is satisfied by it.

( ) The essence of the Universe and essence of all things in it, including the slime mold, you and I, are identical in any moment. We are all the homeostatic GUFA of any moment's time and space attracted to survive, to more strongly, through new attraction diversity, become the next moment of time and space in pure, self-correcting balance.

( ) The non-story GUFA of the Universe includes the life of Planet Earth. Our Planet's life includes your life along with your inherent, attractive, 54-sense way of thinking, feeling, knowing, articulating and building relationships.

( ) The GUFA of everything in the life of Organism Earth's influence only exists in this moment. For this reason, this moment is the only time when any or all of your 54 senses can register, think/feel experience or act from the organic powers of GUAF aliveness in a natural area. This is also true for a Slime Mold. In this way in the web-of-life we are all kin, alive and equal in any moment.

( ) The GUFA homeostatic powers of Organism Earth produce its natural balance and beauty. They purify, self-correct, recycle and transform things so that the peace of Earth's cooperation and diversity sustains itself without producing garbage or misleading story driven assaults including war. For example, these self-balancing attraction ways edit the heat and rays from the sun to promote Earth's life and they also don't let the sea get too salty so that it's not fit for life. Similarly, in our body GUFA regulates our temperature and the salinity of the serum in our blood.

( ) In the GUFA of Planet Earth, only humanity has the gift of being able to articulate, understand and build relationships with our sense of literacy, our abstract story-telling and labeling. The rest our planet is "non-literate." For this reason, the life of Earth is vulnerable to our nature-disconnecting stories and the stress and excessiveness they produce as the tools they make eviscerate GUAF aliveness, in and around us

( ) In this GUFA moment you are guided by *human-built stories* that you often emotionally attach to and think, feel or act with to gain felt-sense satisfactions for your 54 natural senses. You can gain satisfactions from stories that either:

A) **Connect you with** and support the integrity of your self-correcting, 54 sense intelligence and GreenWave-54 whole life powers while in a natural area. As you may have already experienced, moments you spend in Nature enable GUFA as Earth's life help you produce responsible happiness and well-being in and around you in those moments and the moments that follow. (Cohen, 2015).

B) **Disconnect you from the integrity** of your 54 sense intelligence and unifying powers of GUFA as Earth in natural areas and, to your loss, *dis-integrate* responsible happiness in and around you in any moment. This stressful posture continues until this disconnection is corrected by stories in natural areas that re-connect you with GUFA/Earth rather than by additional toxic substitutes for it.

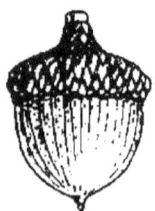**To be fair and provide you with the value of first hand sensory experience with GreenWave-54 for your deliberations** I will have you do one of its nature-connection activities now in this room (Cohen, 2007a). Experience is the best teacher. This is because it involves many senses.

The Nature we will use will be the unified field aliveness of you and the air in this room. Although it was at one time pure, our nature-disconnected stories have made this air far above the safe pollution limits set by the World Health Organization. That infringes upon its and our attraction for it to support life by being pure itself and purifying us.

I used the primary GreenWave-54 *Gaining Consent Activity* (Cohen, 1994), to respect the air here, rather than, as is normal, take it for granted. Earlier, I asked and received permission from the air to do this activity with it for educational purposes. I have in addition thanked it for supporting the Department of Justice's efforts here on behalf of the life of our planet and us.

Too often we forget that when we inhale fresh air, we receive a vital, ancient gift to our lives from our Other Body, the life of non-verbal Planet Earth. Air is a nurturing and unifying present of and by nature's global community, a supportive essence of our ability to live as it surrounds and flows through us.

Do you recognize that when you exhale your breath, the life of Earth breathes you? You breathe out carbon dioxide and water vapor into the air. They are food and water that nurture the plant, animal, mineral and energy world and are attractive to them. Your breath attractively helps to sustain all other forms of life. It is one of your gifts to them. That is attractive, it is the unified field in action.

In earlier times, the word for air was "psyche." Psyche also means spirit and mind.

- *Psychological* can mean "logic or study of the spirit."
- Breathing air is called *respiration,* originally meaning "re-spiriting."
- The word *inspiration* means "bringing air/spirit in."
- The word *expiration* means "letting air/spirit leave."
- When we fully *expire*, we cultural-story "die," lose our name and at the same time transform into other life forms.
- The word *atmosphere* comes from the ancient word for soul.
- The word *conspire* means to unify, to breathe together

For reasonable educational and demonstration purposes here, *please exhale and then hold your breath for a few moments.* Do this now.

While you are holding your breath, recognize it is obvious that you have stopped breathing and have disconnected your GreenWave-54 attraction to the life of air and nature in this regard.

Notice how a sensation is developing in you, a natural feeling attraction, a consciousness of air, a connective natural attraction strand of the web of life to and from air. This uncomfortable but vital desire for air (Senses #25-27) is communicating through a unified field sensory message that increasingly attracts you to breathe again. This is your inherent appetite for air sensation (Sense #21) in action that we sometimes call "suffocation." It is the life of Earth feelingly urging you, attracting you, motivating you to be sane and healthy, to reconnect with the atmosphere and the life of the planet. When you don't, you live with disconnection pain and the disorders that it generates. This is similarly true when we disconnect our 53 other senses from their natural source. That is the time our sense of reason can contribute. (Sense #41)

Do you trust the good intent of this natural attraction feeling and what it is calling you to do? Do you think that it is acting intelligently in a way that benefits all?

 **Even if you faint from lack of air, your natural attraction to air will revive and rejuvenate you by making you breathe again.** That is its "choice," the life of nature's loving, unifying intelligence and unified field operating to provide natural rather than artificial respiration. This attraction-desire to breathe is one of the ways nature works and communicates. It does this because Nature needs and wants you to help sustain the global community so, intelligently, it reconnects you to it, and makes the connection feel attractive and fulfilling to you. It is emotionally rewarding. Nature also does the same thing in different ways for every other member of the life of Earth.

Do you recognize that our obvious felt-sense sensation of "appetite for air" or "suffocation" is not included in the 5-senses that we are indoctrinated to believe are how we know and relate to the world? Does that omission in our education and counseling make sense to you? Isn't it the "sin or lie of omission"?

Let me remind you that as the witnesses here have already testified to you, we and the universe consist of atoms and atoms consist almost entirely of space filled with natural attraction energies. Through natural attraction senses, sensitivities, sensibilities and sensations, nature feelingly "speaks." It communicates its attraction for you to participate in life. You belong and you are it, you are uniquely natural attraction as you. Every few years all the atoms that are you now are attracted to return to the environment/nature and new atoms replace them. You are your special people-being of the attractive dance and flow of 10-billion-year-old atoms from the stars.

Another very obvious and attractive attribute of air that we usually learn to overlook is that it is through the air that we register color, light, forms, scents, sounds, speech, temperature, sunlight, chemicals, clouds, motion, wind and rain. Air is part of our ability to register all these attractions. Is it any wonder that natural people(s) considered air to be part of spirit and soul? What do you think your life would be like if air was black and it did not carry sound or scent?

Begin to breathe normally again if you have not already done so.

Note that when you reconnect with air by breathing, *nature rewards you* for staying alive as part of its life. It gives you an attractive, satisfying, enjoyable good feeling, natural *inspiration* sensation. Nature "invented" that attractive, fulfilling sensation for us (via triggering dopamine, oxycodone, endorphins et al).

Sensation **is a form and part of natural communication**, a sensitivity that is sensible and makes sense. Do you think you trust that your good-feeling sensation from inhaling now is real and is valid, that its existence is a fact, just like the existence of air is also a fact? Does it make sense to omit this fact in our education and the "objective science" process? Do you recognize the disorders that result from not doing so?

Through this natural sensation reward, the life of Earth expresses its appreciation for your supportive participation. Without using words, the sensation thanks you for reconnecting. It thanks you for your natural gifts of carbon dioxide and water vapor to the global community. They could not survive without this gift from you and others. And you could not survive without their gifts to you. Such attractive, mutually beneficial, cooperative support is an essence of how nature works, from sub-atomics to solar systems, from the Big Bang to this moment. (Sense #54). It is also purifying and restorative as it *conspires* with 53 other senses to recycle our body mind and spirit. This is sensible, it makes sense.

Note that now after sharing with each other what you experienced during the activity, you feel happier, stronger and more united than before. You are more resilient and more open to change. ***You will never be the same again because this moment's senses,*** *story and chemistry are now the Unified Field as you forever. In addition, as behavioral epigenetics show, your children will inherit this quality from you.*

Do you trust or celebrate this attractive and rewarding feeling of thanks from nature and the ancient life relationship it brings to mind? It is communication and connection with all of life including your neighbors. It is with you, and part of you, all of your life, your non-verbal "Other Body." It is an empirical fact that is always there for you. Do you think it deserves your respect, attention, trust and gratitude?

It is reasonable for us and the environment to breathe together, to communicate, to cooperatively connect. The rewards from this attractive, mutually beneficial "love" relationship help us reduce our "unchangeable addictions and disconnections," as well as support and sustain our life and all of life. Although we can't see it, we can sense that it is intelligent, right and it feels good.

Does it make sense and have value to you that you have just GreenWave-54 grokked the air?

Note that it is perfectly legal and justified for this jury to 54 sense *conspire* **with the life of the unified field in the planet, people and each other** to bring to trial the defendants in this inquest. Doing this will stop the latter from depriving us of our inalienable human rights to life and information. It will help the public similarly conspire and use 160 additional organic GreenWave activities and 46 more senses to unite and remedy the runaway personal, social and environmental challenges that overwhelm us because we are excessively disconnected from Nature's wisdom.

Who does this jury think is going to help us control our juggernauting automobile if the Defendants have denied us the ability to accept scientifically valid GreenWave-54 assistance that is available? Please read this scientific article (Cohen, 2017). Make the right decision and use it to safely reach the folks we need.

We will break for lunch now and reconvene at 1:30 this afternoon.

Things you can do:

Readers of this book are invited to

1)   Submit questions about the GreenWave and testimony that will be answered in an additional book that reports the proceedings of the investigation as it continues. Email your questions to nature@interisland.net

2)   Become members of its Grand Jury and help it reach its conclusion by taking on the role of an online juror as additional witnesses testify.

3)   Become an additional witness expert and submit your testimony.

4)   Become a member of the class action against the defendants.

5)   Become a supporter of the class action suit process.

6)   Learn and teach GreenWave-54 to others as a livelihood or hobby in a class that is starting in a week or two online at www.ecopsych.com/orient.html

7)   Become GreenWave literate via www.mjcnow.info and its links.

Read GreenWave-54 via www.mjcnow.info, draw your own conclusions and contact Dr. Cohen at 360-378-6313 nature@interisland.net Simply submit "Yes for trial" or "No for trial" or your own Witness Statement, or a supportive statement.

This book will be used to help a kick start publication and an application of *Romancing Our Planet: Albert Einstein's Unified Field GreenWave Guide to Personal and Global Well Being* along with do it yourself methods and materials for actualizing it. Contact 360-378-6313 nature@interisland.net to participate in this challenge and receive a free copy of the forthcoming publication and application.

Additional comments, proposals and updates to this indictment are located at www.ecopsych.com/grandjury22.html

Onward

Once you have completed this book, you are invited to learn and teach GreenWave-54 (www.mjcnow.info)(www.ecopsych.com/orient.html) or enjoy consciously being the unified field and its natural attraction energies, [as described by Steve Recter, (witness 27 page 57.) and www.ProjectNatureConnect.net.] Simply follow these steps:

1. From your attraction to a natural area's GreenWave Unified Field Aliveness (GUFA), backyard or back country, gain consent for your aliveness to visit it supportively; convey that it is attractive to you not to harm it. If it remains attractive and is safe, its aliveness has consented to your proposal. If not, try again later or find another area. (See www.ecopsych.com/amental.html for details and additional activities.)

2. Find a natural attraction in this area that remains attractive for more than seven seconds, (a cloud, the wind, a flower, a color or design etc.). That attraction will support you as you continue because what you are attracted to is what is making it attractive in this moment.

3. One by one, with or without using the list in the Appendix, find other natural attractions in the area and accurately label them as the senses that they are on the list. For example, it is factual to call your attraction for drinking water, "thirst," for that helps translate it correctly into our story world.

4. When possible do this activity with others who have read this book. Share your thoughts and feelings about what happens with them as you do it. Can you find commonality and unity through your shared conscious connections with the Unified Field?

   Can you do this same activity with the "natural area" being the natural aliveness in another person? What happens when you apply some of the 54 attraction list senses to the Unified Field personified as that individual?

Please contact me if you want course credit for doing 1-4.

Mike Cohen, Ph.D.
P. O. Box 1605 Friday Harbor WA 98250   (360) 378-6313
www.ecopsych.com nature@interisland.net

References

A new Copernicun revolution. (2012). *Journal of Organic Psychology and Natural Attraction Ecology, 2.* *Retrieved from* http://www.ecopsych.com/journalcopernicus.html

Alban, D. (2016) *Epigenetics: How you can change Your Genes and Change Your Life.* Retrieved from http://reset.me/story/epigenetics-how-you-can-change-your-genes-and-change-your-life/

Albert Einstein's unified field equation. (2014-2016). *Journal of Organic Psychology and Natural Attraction Ecology, 2.*
Retrieved from http://www.ecopsych.com/einsteinstart.html

Block, J. (2016) *First in Nation Lawsuit Over Climate Change.* Retrieved from http://www.clf.org/newsroom/clf-files-lawsuit-against-exxonmobil/

Brown, N. (1990). *Love's body.* University of California Press.

Cohen, M. J. (1983). Prejudice Against Nature. *Cobblesmith.*
Retrieved from http://www.ecopsych.com/prejudicebigotry.html

Cohen, M. J. (1993). *The training ground of a nature-connected expert.* (2014). Retrieved from http://www.ecopsych.com/mjcohen.html

Cohen, M. J. (1994) *The global wellness and unity activity.* Retrieved from http://www.ecopsych.com/amental.html

Cohen, M. J. (1995). Education and counseling with nature: A greening of psychotherapy. *The Interspsych Newsletter, 2*(4). Retrieved from http://www.ecopsych.com/counseling.html

Cohen, M. J. (2007a). *Thinking and feeling, and relating through the joy of nature's perfection.* Retrieved from http://www.ecopsych.com/naturepath.html

Cohen, M. J. (2007b). *Whom am I? Who or what is your natural self?* Retrieved from http://www.ecopsych.com/thesisquote6.html

Cohen, M. J. (2008). *Educating, counseling, and healing with nature.* Illumina. Retrieved from http://www.ecopsych.com/ksanity.html

Cohen, M. J. (2009a). *How to transform destructive thinking into constructive relationships.* Retrieved from http://www.ecopsych.com/transformation.html

Cohen, M. J. (2011). *The anatomy of institutions.* Retrieved from http://www.ecopsych.com/journalinstitution.html

Cohen, M. J. (2012). *The Slime Mold Alternative.* Retrieved from http://www.ecopsych.com/journalslimemold.html

Cohen, M. J. (2013). *The great sensory equation dance.* Retrieved from http://www.ecopsych.com/journalgut.html

Cohen, M. J. (2014). *Benefit from consciously registering your fifty-four natural senses.* Retrieved from http://www.ecopsych.com/insight53senses.html

Cohen, M. J. (2015). *A Survey of Nature-connected learning participants.* Retrieved from http://www.ecopsych.com/survey.html

Cohen, M. J. (2016). *Maverick Genius Walk.* Retrieved from http://www.ecopsych.com/MAKESENSEWALK.docx

Cohen, M. J. (2017) *The Missing Element in Unsolvable Problems: Attraction is Conscious of What it is Attracted to.* Retrieved from http://www.ecopsych.com/GREENWAVE.docx

Dewey, J. (1934). Individual psychology and education. *The Philosopher, 2.* Retrieved http://www.ascd.org/ASCD/pdf/journals/ed_update/eu201207_infographic.pdf

Doherty, T. J. (2010). Michael Cohen: Ecopsychology interview. *Ecopsychology Journal, 2.* Retrieved from http://www.ecopsych.com/ecopsychologyjournal.html

Einstein, A., Cohen, M.J. (2014-2016)). Albert Einstein's unified field equation. *Journal of Organic Psychology and Natural Attraction Ecology, 2.*
Retrieved from http://www.ecopsych.com/einsteinstart.html

Fishman, K. (1854). Chief Seattle's speech. *Wildwood Survival.* Retrieved from http://www.wildwoodsurvival.com/wildernessmind/chiefseattle.html

Grange [#966]. (2015). Resolutions.Retrieved from http://www.sjigrange.wordpress.com/resolutions

Green, B. (2013). How the Higgs Boson was found. *Smithsonian Magazine.* Retrieved from http://www.smithsonianmag.com/science-nature/how-the-higgs-boson-was-f und 4723520/?cmd=ChdjYS1wdWItMjY0NDQyNTI0NTE5MDk0Nw&page=3

Hoke, P. (2015) Maverick Genius at Work. Retrieved from http://www.ecopsych.com/maverick-genius

Holthaus, E. (2016) *Kids Suing Government Over Climate Change.* Retrieved from http://www.slate.com/articles/health_and_science/science/2016/11/the_kids_lawsuit_over_climate_ch ange_is_our_best_hope_now.html

Kluger, J. (2014). *The sixth great extinction.* Time Magazine. Retrieved from http://time.com/3035872/sixth-great-extinction/

Milgram, (1974). Obedience to authority: An experimental view. Harpercollins. Retrieved from https://en.wikipedia.org/wiki/Milgram_experiment

Pascal, B. (1995). *Pensées.* (p. 312). Oxford University Press, USA.: Penguin Books Retrieved from http://www.naturalchild.org/jan_hunt/babyspeaks.html

Skinner, B.F. (1971) *Beyond Freedom & Dignity,* Pelican Books. Retrieved from http://selfdefinition.org/psychology/BF-Skinner-Beyond Freedom-&-Dignity-1971.pdf

Robinson, T.N. (2007) *Effects of Fast Food Branding on Young Children's Taste Preferences* Journal of the American Medical Association   Retrieved from http://jamanetwork.com/journals/jamapediatrics/fullarticle/570933

International Astronomical Union. (2015). *Universe is dying.* Retrieved from http://news.discovery.com/space/galaxies/universe-is-dying-galactic-survey-shows-150810.htm

Natural attraction ecology. (2003). Retrieved from http://www.naturalattractionecology.com/index.html#anchoraxiom

Our living universe: Who is the boss of you? (2014). Retrieved from http://www.ecopsych.com/universealive.html

Peak fact: Whole life self evidence in action. (2010). *Journal of Organic Psychology and Natural Attraction Ecology, 2.* Retrieved from http://www.ecopsych.com/journalpeak.html

Project NatureConnect (PNC). (1997). *Reconnecting With Nature,* EcoPress. Retrieved from http://www.ecopsych.com/insight53senses.html

The hidden organic remedy: Nature as higher power. (2013). *Journal of Organic Psychology and Natural Attraction Ecology, 1.* Retrieved from http://www.ecopsych.com/nhpbook.html

The impossible dream: We ask you to be a part of it. (2011-2013). *Journal of Organic Psychology and Natural Attraction Ecology, 1.* Retrieved from http://www.ecopsych.com/journalwarranty.html

The magic of something from nothing. (2012). Journal of Organic Psychology and Natural Attraction Ecology, 2. Retrieved from http://www.ecopsych.com/journalessence.html

The National Grange. (1874, February 11). The declaration of purposes of the National Grange, Retrieved from http://www.oocities.org/cannongrange/declaration_purposes.html

The state of planet earth and us. (2001). Retrieved from http://www.ecopsych.com/zombie2.html

Thinking and learning with all nine legs. (2011). Retrieved from   http://www.ecopsych.com/nineleg.html

Who, what or when is the acronym NNIAAL? (2013). Retrieved from http://www.ecopsych.com/earthstories101.html

Searls, D. (2009). The Journal of Henry David Thoreau, 1837-1861 December 6 entry, New York Review Books Classics. Retrieved from https://en.wikiquote.org/wiki/Henry_David_Thoreau

APPENDIX

OUR FIFTY-FOUR NATURAL SENSES AND SENSITIVITIES

This list explains how, sense by sense in 54-sense resonance, the GreenWave natural attraction Unified Field (GreenWave-54) connects with and unifies itself in us, through us and with people and places around us. By putting these senses into scientific stories and labels the list enables our sense of language(#39) to consciously(#42) and reasonably(#43) translate into and engage in reasonable stories that connect us to the life and love of Nature/Earth's moment-by-moment, self-correcting survival process(#54). GreenWave-54 is the outcome of the author's 51 years of living this organic experience in natural area space and time that includes his trained, evidence-based knowledge and awareness.
(see www.ecopsych.com/insight53senses.html)

The Radiation Senses

1. Sense of height and sight, including polarized light.
2. Sense of seeing without eyes such as heliotropism or the sun sense of plants.
3. Sense of color.
4. Sense of moods and identities attached to colors.
5. Sense of awareness of one's own visibility or invisibility and consequent camouflaging.
6. Sensitivity to radiation other than visible light including radio waves, X rays, etc.
7. Sense of Temperature and temperature change.
8. Sense of season including ability to insulate, hibernate and winter sleep.
9. Electromagnetic sense and polarity which includes the ability to generate current (as in the nervous system and brain waves) or other energies.

The Feeling Senses

10. Hearing including resonance, vibrations, sonar and ultrasonic frequencies.
11. Awareness of pressure, particularly underground, underwater, and to wind and air.
12. Sensitivity to gravity.
13. The sense of excretion for waste elimination and protection from enemies.
14. Feel, particularly touch on the skin.
15. Sense of weight, gravity and balance.
16. Space or proximity sense.
17. Coriolus sense or awareness of effects of the rotation of the Earth.
18. Sense of motion. Body movement sensations and sense of mobility.

The Chemical Senses

19. Smell with and beyond the nose.
20. Taste with and beyond the tongue.
21. Appetite or hunger for food, water and air.
22. Hunting, killing or food obtaining urges.
23. Humidity sense including thirst, evaporation control and the acumen to find water or evade a flood.
24. Hormonal sense, as to pheromones and other chemical stimuli.

The Mental Senses.

(25-27 attractions that convey *seek additional natural attractions* to support well-being).

25. **Pain, external and internal.**

26. **Mental or spiritual distress.**

27. **Sense of fear, dread of injury, death or attack**

28. Procreative urges: sex awareness, courting, love, mating, paternity and raising young.

29. Sense of play, sport, humor, pleasure and laughter.

30. Sense of physical place, navigation senses including detailed awareness of land and seascapes, of the positions of the sun, moon and stars.

31. Sense of time and rhythm.

32. Sense of electromagnetic fields.

33. Sense of weather changes.

34. Sense of emotional place, of community, belonging, support, trust and thankfulness.

35. Sense of self including friendship, companionship, and power.

36. Domineering and territorial sense.

37. Colonizing sense including compassion and receptive awareness of ones fellow creatures, sometimes to the degree of being absorbed into a superorganism.

38. Horticultural sense and the ability to cultivate crops, as is done by ants that grow fungus, by fungus who farm algae, or birds that leave food to attract their prey.

39. **Language and articulation sense,** used to express feelings and convey information in every medium from the bees' dance to human stories and literature.

40. Sense of humility, appreciation, ethics.

41. Senses of form and design.

42. **Sense of reason,** including memory and the capacity for logic and science.

43. **Sense of mind and consciousness.**

44. Intuition or subconscious deduction.

45. Aesthetic sense, including creativity and appreciation of beauty, music, literature, form, design and drama.

46. Psychic capacity such as foreknowledge, clairvoyance, clairaudience, psychokinesis, astral projection and possibly certain animal instincts and plant sensitivities.

47. Sense of biological and astral time, awareness of past, present and future events.

48. The capacity to hypnotize other creatures.

49. Relaxation and sleep including dreaming, meditation, brain wave awareness.

50. Sense of pupation including cocoon building and metamorphosis.

51. Sense of excessive stress and capitulation.

52. Sense of survival by joining a more established organism.

53. Spiritual sense, including conscience, capacity for sublime love, ecstasy, a sense of sin, profound sorrow and sacrifice

54. Sense of unity, of natural attraction as the singular mother essence of all our other senses *(and everything else that singularity was and remains attracted to create, unify and support moment-by-moment as the Big Bang Unified Field-Higgs Boson that was verified in 2012 A.D.).*

Summary of Witness Testimonies

By 85 percent GreenWave-54

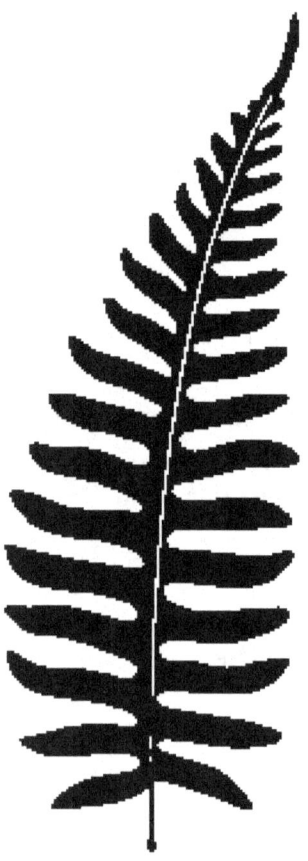

- improves the quality, rights and well-being of life.
- strengthens our ability to make beneficial changes.
- enhances equality through wholeness.
- bolsters appropriateness of education.
- reinforces the scientific truth of natural love.
- increases love and common good to stop corruption.
- heightens self-appreciation and sensory awareness.
- strengthens our trust in scientific methodology.
- strengthens whole life equality.
- enhances pain reduction.
- reduces fear, negativity and depression.
- intensifies harmony and our right to be loved.
- supports personal and global aliveness.
- strengthens the sense and vision of unity
- increases intelligent attraction consciousness.
- restores the wisdom of reasonable happiness.
- affirms our right to demand whole life facts anywhere.
- sustains us lovingly communicating with the eons.
- reinforces our safe personal rejuvenation.
- invigorates organically based critical thinking.
- supports my healing attraction to emotional place.
- unchains our inborn ability to love all of life.
- reverses our trespasses of Nature in and around us.
- heightens self-nourishing and supportive energies.
- reduces our addictive prejudice against Nature.
- empowers recuperation from post-traumatic stress.
- enables sensing ourselves as the Unified Field.
- institutionally increases people/planet sanity